# Beginning Arduino Nano 33 IoT

## Step-By-Step Internet of Things Projects

Agus Kurniawan

Apress®

*Beginning Arduino Nano 33 IoT: Step-By-Step Internet of Things Projects*

Agus Kurniawan
Faculty of Computer Science, Universitas Indonesia
Depok, Indonesia

ISBN-13 (pbk): 978-1-4842-6445-4          ISBN-13 (electronic): 978-1-4842-6446-1
https://doi.org/10.1007/978-1-4842-6446-1

Managing Director, Apress Media LLC: Welmoed Spahr
Acquisitions Editor: Natalie Pao
Development Editor: James Markham
Coordinating Editor: Jessica Vakili

Distributed to the book trade worldwide by Springer Science+Business Media New York, 1 NY Plaza, New York, NY 10014. Phone 1-800-SPRINGER, fax (201) 348-4505, e-mail orders-ny@springer-sbm.com, or visit www.springeronline.com. Apress Media, LLC is a California LLC and the sole member (owner) is Springer Science + Business Media Finance Inc (SSBM Finance Inc). SSBM Finance Inc is a **Delaware** corporation.

For information on translations, please e-mail booktranslations@springernature.com; for reprint, paperback, or audio rights, please e-mail bookpermissions@springernature.com.

Apress titles may be purchased in bulk for academic, corporate, or promotional use. eBook versions and licenses are also available for most titles. For more information, reference our Print and eBook Bulk Sales web page at http://www.apress.com/bulk-sales.

Any source code or other supplementary material referenced by the author in this book is available to readers on GitHub via the book's product page, located at www.apress.com/978-1-4842-6445-4. For more detailed information, please visit http://www.apress.com/source-code.

Printed on acid-free paper

# Table of Contents

# About the Author

**Agus Kurniawan** is a lecturer, IT consultant, and author. He has 15 years of experience in various software and hardware development projects, delivering materials in training and workshops, and technical writing. He has been awarded the Microsoft Most Valuable Professional (MVP) award 14 years in a row.

Agus is a lecturer and researcher in the field of networking and security systems at the Faculty of Computer Science, Universitas Indonesia, Indonesia. Currently, he is pursuing a PhD in computer science at the Freie Universität in Berlin, Germany. He can be reached on Twitter at @agusk2010.

# About the Technical Reviewer

**Mike McRoberts** is the author of *Beginning Arduino* by Apress. He is winner of Pi Wars 2018 and member of Medway Makers. He is an Arduino and Raspberry Pi enthusiast.

C/C++, Arduino, Python, Processing, JS, Node-Red, NodeJS, Lua.

# CHAPTER 1

# Setting up Development Environment

Arduino Nano 33 IoT is an internet of things (IoT) solution to perform sensing and actuating on physical environment. The Arduino Nano 33 IoT board comes with WiFi and BLE modules that enable communication with other entities for exchanging data. This chapter will explore how to set up the Arduino Nano 33 IoT board for development.

The following is a list of topics in this chapter:

- Reviewing Arduino Nano 33 IoT board

- Setting up development environment

- Building LED blinking program

- Applying Arduino web editor

© Agus Kurniawan 2021
A. Kurniawan, *Beginning Arduino Nano 33 IoT*,
https://doi.org/10.1007/978-1-4842-6446-1_1

# Introduction

Arduino Nano 33 IoT is one of IoT platforms from Arduino. This board uses WiFi and Bluetooth modules to connect to a network. WiFi is a common network that people use to access Internet. Bluetooth is a part of wireless personal network (WPAN) that enables communication with other devices within a short distance.

Arduino Nano 33 IoT board is designed for low-cost IoT devices to address your IoT problems. Arduino Nano 33 IoT has a small-size factor, 45 x 18 mm (length x width). You can see my Arduino Nano 33 IoT board in Figure 1-1.

***Figure 1-1.*** *Arduino Nano 33 IoT board*

# Review Arduino Nano 33 IoT Board

Arduino Nano 33 IoT is built from ARM Cortex M0 32-bit SAMD21. The board also has a radio module, NINA-W102, from u-blox. This module is designed for data communication over WiFi and Bluetooth. You can read a detailed specification of Arduino Nano 33 IoT on Table 1-1.

Since Arduino Nano 33 IoT has some digital and analog I/O, we extend the board capabilities by wiring with other sensors or actuators. We also use universal asynchronous receiver/transmitter (UART), serial peripheral interface (SPI), and interintergrated circuit (I2C) protocols to communicate with other devices.

***Table 1-1.*** *A Specification of Arduino Nano 33 IoT*

| Features | Notes |
| --- | --- |
| Microcontroller | SAMD21 Cortex-M0+ 32-bit |
| Radio module | u-blox NINA-W102 |
| Secure module | ATECC608A |
| Operating voltage | 3.3V |
| Input voltage | 21V |
| DC current per I/O pin (limit) | 7 mA |
| Clock speed | 48 Mhz |
| CPU flash memory | 256 KB |
| SRAM | 32 KB |
| EEPROM | None |
| Digital I/O | 14 |
| PWM pins | 11 (2, 3, 5, 6, 9, 10, 11, 12, 16 / A2, 17 / A3, 19 / A5) |

(*continued*)

***Table 1-1.*** *(continued)*

| Features | Notes |
|---|---|
| UART | 1 |
| SPI | 1 |
| I2C | 1 |
| Analog Input | 8 (ADC 8/10/12 bit) |
| Analog Output | 1 (DAC 10 bit) |
| LED_BUILTIN | 13 |
| USB | Native in the SAMD21 processor |
| IMU | LSM6DS3 |
| Size (Length x Width) | 45 mm x 18 mm |

*Key: CPU, central processing unit; SRAM, static random-access memory; EEPROM, electrically erasable programmable read-only memory; PWM, pulse width modulation; UART, universal asynchronous receiver/transmitter; SPI, serial peripheral interfact; I2C, interintergrated circuit; USB, universal serial bus; IMU, inertial measurement unit.*

Next, we will set up Arduino Nano 33 IoT on your computer so you can build programs for Arduino board.

# Set Up Development Environment

Arduino provides software to build programs for all Arduino board models. We can use Arduino software. You can download Arduino software on the following link: https://www.arduino.cc/en/Main/Software. This software is available for Windows, Linux, and macOS.

The installation process steps are easy. Just follow the installation guideline from Arduino setup. After finished installation, you will see the Arduino application menu on main menu from your OS platform.

Open the Arduino application. Then, we will obtain the Arduino application as shown in Figure 1-2. You will see skeleton codes on the application dialog. The following is a code template.

```
void setup() {
  // put your setup code here, to run once:
}

void loop() {
  // put your main code here, to run repeatedly:
}
```

We can see that the Arduino program adopts C/C++ program language dialects. We can put all data initialization on the setup() function. The program will execute codes inside the loop() function continuously.

***Figure 1-2.***  *Arduino software for Windows*

To work with the Arduino Nano 33 IoT board, we need to configure Arduino software. First, we add Arduino SAMD Boards so the Arduino software will recognize our Arduino Nano 33 IoT board. You can open a menu on Arduino software by clicking the menu **Tools ➤ Board … ➤ Boards Manager…**

After clicking the Board Manager menu, we will obtain the Boards Manager dialog, as shown in Figure 1-3. Select All on the Type menu from Boards Manager. Then, type Arduino&NANO&33&IoT in the textbox. You will see Arduino SAMD Boards. Click and install this package. Make sure your computer is connected to an Internet network.

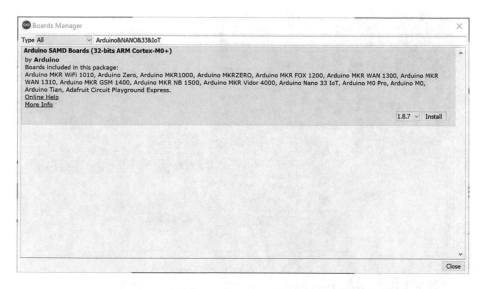

***Figure 1-3.*** *Adding supported boards for Arduino Nano 33 IoT*

This installation takes several minutes to complete. After completed installation, you can see the Arduino Nano 33 IoT board on the targeted board. You can verify it by clicking the menu **Tools ➤ Board ... ➤ Boards Manager...**on Arduino software. You will see your board list. Figure 1-4 shows Arduino Nano 33 IoT on Arduino software.

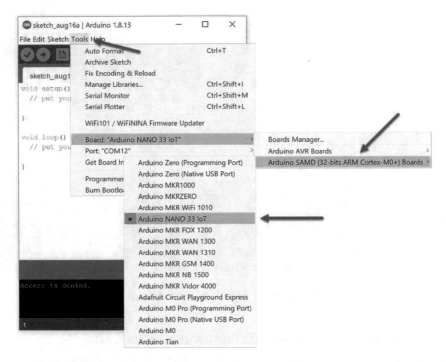

**Figure 1-4.** *A list of targeted boards for Arduino*

Now you attach Arduino Nano 33 IoT to a computer via micro USB cable. After attached, you can verify your board using Device Manager for Windows. Figure 1-5 shows my Arduino Nano 33 IoT on Windows 10.

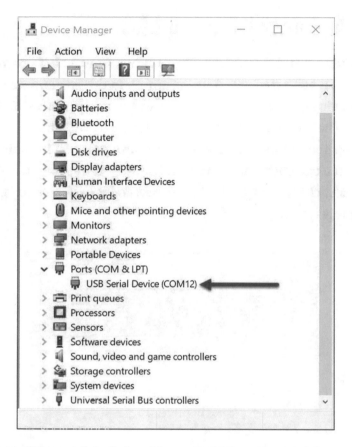

**Figure 1-5.** *Detected Arduino Nano 33 IoT on Device Manager—Windows 10*

If you are working on Linux, you can verify the Arduino Nano 33 IoT using this command on the terminal.

```
$ ls /dev/ttyUSB*
```

You will see a list of attached devices over USB. Arduino Nano 33 IoT usually is detected as /dev/ttyUSB0 or */dev/ttyUSB1*. For macOS, you can type this command to check Arduino Nano 33 IoT.

```
$ ls /dev/cu*
```

You should see the USB device on your terminal.

# Hello Arduino: Blinking LED

We first build a Arduino program. The Arduino Nano 33 IoT board has a built-in LED that is attached on digital pin 13. In this section, we build a simple blinking LED. Now you can connect Arduino Nano 33 IoT into a computer. Then, we can start to write the Arduino program.

You can open Arduino software. We create a program from the project template. You can click menu and then File ➤ Examples ➤ 01.Basics ➤ Blink. After clicked, you will obtain program codes as shown in Figure 1-6. This is a program sample from Arduino.

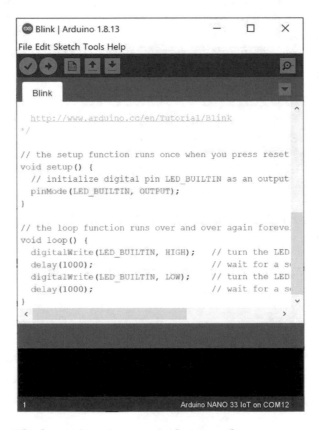

***Figure 1-6.*** *Blink application on Arduino software*

You can see the program codes are written as follows.

```
void setup() {
  // initialize digital pin LED_BUILTIN as an output.
  pinMode(LED_BUILTIN, OUTPUT);
}

// the loop function runs over and over again forever
void loop() {
  digitalWrite(LED_BUILTIN, HIGH);    // turn the LED on (HIGH
                                      is the voltage level)
  delay(1000);                        // wait for a second
  digitalWrite(LED_BUILTIN, LOW);     // turn the LED off by
                                      making the voltage LOW
  delay(1000);                        // wait for a second
}
```

Save this program. Now we can compile and upload the Arduino program into Arduino Nano 33 IoT. You can click the Verify icon to compile the Arduino program. To upload the Arduino program into the board, click the Upload icon on Arduino software. You can see these icons in Figure 1-7.

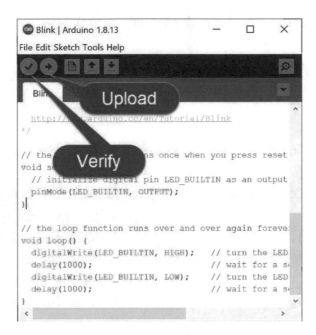

**Figure 1-7.**  *Compiling and flashing a program*

After uploading the Arduino program into Arduino Nano 33 IoT, we will see blinking LED on the Arduino Nano 33 IoT board. You can see my blinking LED in Figure 1-8.

***Figure 1-8.*** *Blinking LED on Arduino Nano 33 IoT*

How does it work?

Arduino Nano 33 IoT board has one built-in LED on digital pin 13. In our program, we set digital pin 13 as digital output using pinMode(). We initialize this data on the setup() function.

```
void setup() {
  // initialize digital pin LED_BUILTIN as an output.
  pinMode(LED_BUILTIN, OUTPUT);
}
```

The Arduino program defines LED_BUILTIN for a general of built-in LED pin. We can set the pin as output mode by giving a value, OUTPUT.

Now our program will run continuously on the loop() function. We turn on LED and then turn off the LED. We can use digitalWrite() to perform on/off on the LED. Set the value to HIGH to turn on the LED. Otherwise, we can turn off the LED by sending a value of LOW on the digitalWrite() function. We also set a delay for turning the LED on/off. We set 1000 ms on the delay() function.

```
void loop() {
  digitalWrite(LED_BUILTIN, HIGH);    // turn the LED on (HIGH
                                         is the voltage level)
  delay(1000);                        // wait for a second
  digitalWrite(LED_BUILTIN, LOW);     // turn the LED off by
                                         making the voltage LOW
  delay(1000);                        // wait for a second
}
```

You can practice the blinking LED program.

Next, we can use the Arduino web editor for alternative tools for Arduino development. We just need a browser and Internet access.

# Arduino Web Editor

Arduino provides an online editor to build Arduino programs. The advantage of online editor is that we don't prepare too many runtimes and tools. We only need a browser and Internet connection.

We can access the Arduino web editor using any browser. You can navigate to the link https://create.arduino.cc/editor. Figure 1-9 shows the Arduino web editor model. To use Arduino web editor, we must register in the Arduino portal to build the Arduino program.

In this section, we will focus on getting started with Arduino web editor. We will perform these tasks to complete our Arduino development with online web editor:

- Register your Arduino portal account

- Install Arduino plug-in

- Build blink application for Arduino Nano 33 IoT

***Figure 1-9.***   *Arduino web editor*

# Registering an Arduino Account

To use and build the Arduino program with Arduino web editor, we must register an Arduino account. This account is a similar account to that used to buy the Arduino board in the Arduino store.

You can register a new Arduino account on the right-top menu icon. You can fill personal information through this portal. After completed account registration, we can build the Arduino program with Arduino web editor.

# Installing Arduino Plug-in

To enable our Arduino Nano 33 IoT to connect to Arduino web editor, we need to install the Arduino plug-in. This is a required task for Windows. The Arduino plug-in will act as a bridge between local Arduino Nano 33 IoT and the Arduino web editor.

First, we open a browser and navigate to the link `https://create.` `arduino.cc/getting-started/plugin/welcome`. Then, we have a form, as shown in Figure 1-10.

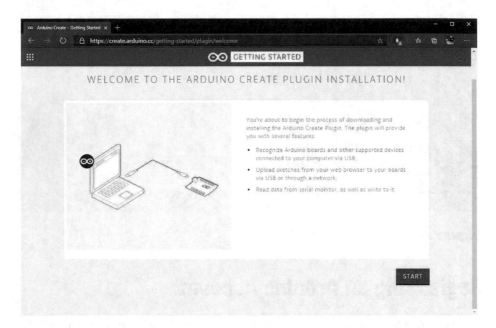

***Figure 1-10.*** *Arduino plug-in installation*

Click the START button. After that, you will see a form, as shown in Figure 1-11. Click the DOWNLOAD button to download the Arduino plug-in application.

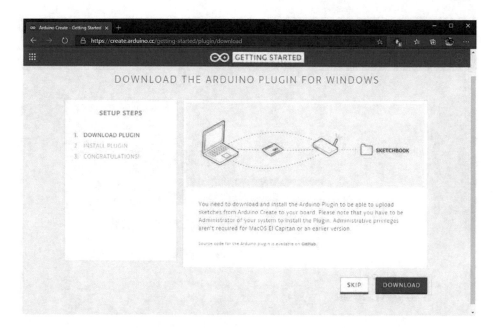

***Figure 1-11.***  *Download the Arduino plug-in for Windows*

After downloading the Arduino plug-in, we can install this application. Follow the installation steps from the setup file. If we finished the Arduino plug-in installation, the browser will detect our Arduino plug-in. Figure 1-12 shows the browser detecting the Arduino plug-in. Click the NEXT button to continue.

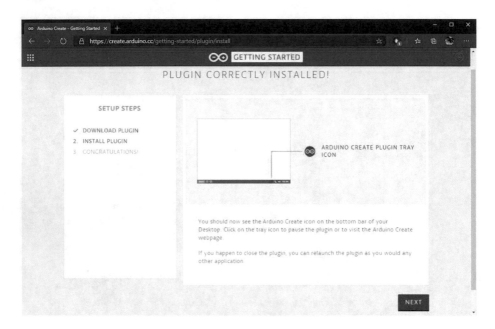

***Figure 1-12.*** *Detecting the Arduino plug-in*

After we click the NEXT button, we receive confirmation of the completed installation, as shown in Figure 1-13.

You can click the GO TO WEB EDITORS button to continue. You will be directed to the Arduino web editor, as shown in Figure 1-9.

Now we are ready for Arduino development using the Arduino web editor. Next, we will build a blink Arduino application.

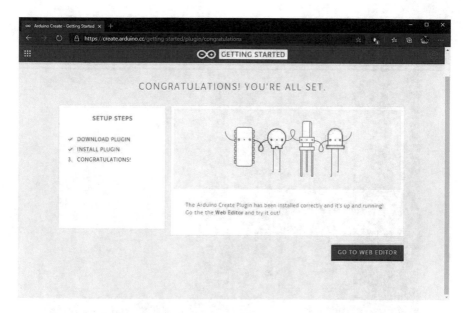

**Figure 1-13.** *Completed Arduino plug-in installation*

# Building an Arduino Program

The Arduino web editor has the same functionalities as the desktop version ofArduino software. The Arduino web editor has project samples. We also can add Arduino libraries into the project.

In this section, we build a blink Arduino application like in the previous project. We start by opening a browser and navigating to https://create.arduino.cc/editor. Click the Examples menu on the left menus. Then, click the BUILTIN tab and select 01.BASICS(6) -> Blink. You can see Figure 1-14 for our Arduino project.

After we select the Blink project sample, we have a blink program. You can see this program in Figure 1-15. Now we can compile and upload the program into Arduino Nano 33 IoT.

Select your Arduino Nano 33 IoT board from the dropdown of the device list. Click the Verify and Upload icon on the left of dropdown. This tool will compile and upload the Arduino program into the targeted board.

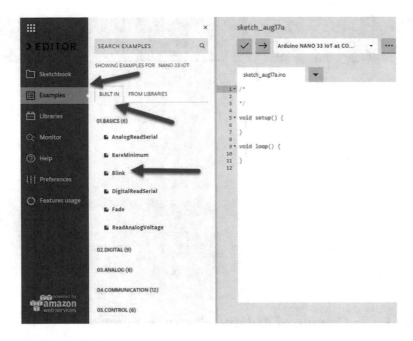

**Figure 1-14.**  *Create a new project*

**Figure 1-15.**  *Uploading a program into Arduino Nano 33 IoT*

We can try to build another Arduino project using the Arduino web editor. We can use project samples from this tool.

This is the end of the chapter for setting up an Arduino development environment.

# Summary

We have learned to set up an Arduino development environment. We also installed Arduino software on a desktop environment. We built a simple Arduino program, blink. In addition, we tried to use the Arduino web editor to build Arduino programs.

Next, we will learn how to access Arduino Nano 33 IoT input/output. We use other communication protocols too.

# CHAPTER 2

# Arduino Nano 33 IoT Board Development

This chapter focuses on how to build Arduino Nano 33 IoT programs. We use Arduino Sketch to build Arduino programs. This software is available for Windows, macOS, and Linux. Then, we explore how to access Input/Output peripherals on the Arduino Nano 33 IoT board by the Arduino program.

In this chapter, you will learn:

- how to write Arduino programs using Sketch
- how to access digital I/O
- how to access analog I/O
- how to plot analog sensor analog
- how to build a serial communication
- how to access PWM
- how to access SPI
- how to scan an I2C address
- how to read sensor device-based I2C

© Agus Kurniawan 2021
A. Kurniawan, *Beginning Arduino Nano 33 IoT*,
https://doi.org/10.1007/978-1-4842-6446-1_2

# Introduction

We can say Arduino is a platform since Arduino as a company provides hardware and software. To build programs for Arduino Nano 33 IoT boards, we can use Arduino Sketch. This program uses C/C++ dialects as its language style.

In this chapter, we learn how to build programs for Arduino Nano 33 IoT. This is one of various Arduino models. The Arduino Nano 33 IoT board uses WiFi and Bluetooth modules to connect to a network. WiFi is a common network that people use to access Internet. Bluetooth is a part of wireless personal network (WPAN) that enables communication with other device in short distance.

We use Arduino software to build Arduino programs. This tool uses the Sketch program that uses C++ dialects. In the next section, we start to learn Sketch programming.

# Basic Sketch Programming

In this section, we learn about Sketch programming language. Technically, Sketch uses C++ dialects, so if you have experience with C++ programming language, you can skip this section.

## Main Program

The Arduino program has a main program to perform tasks continuously. When we create a program using Arduino software, we have skeleton codes with two functions: `setup()` and `loop()`. You can see the complete codes as follows.

```
void setup() {
  // put your setup code here, to run once:

}
```

```
void loop() {
  // put your main code here, to run repeatedly:

}
```

In these codes, we have two functions, setup() and loop(). The setup() function is called once when the Arduino board is turned on. If we put codes in the setup() function, it means our codes will run once. Otherwise, we have the loop() function that is called continuously.

This is a basic of the main program from Arduino. In this section, we learn Sketch programming with the following topics:

- Declaring variables

- Making a conditional statement

- Making loops

- Working with break and continue

Next, we start by declaring variables on the Sketch program.

## Declare Variables

We can declare a variable using the following statement.

```
<data type> <variable name>;
```

<data type> is a keyword from the Sketch program that is adopted from the C++ program. <data type> represents how to define our data type on the variable. <variable name> is the variable name we will call and use in our program. A list of <data type> in the Sketch program can be seen in Table 2-1.

Since the Sketch program adopts from C++, we put ; at the end of the code line. Otherwise, we obtain an error while compiling codes. For instance, we declare variables with int and char data types as follows:

```
int a;
int b = 10;
char c;
char d = 'A';
```

We can set an initial value while declaring a variable. For instance, we set int b = 10.

***Table 2-1.*** *Data Types on the Sketch Program*

| | | |
|---|---|---|
| array | float | void |
| bool | int | String() |
| Boolean | long | unsigned char |
| Byte | short | unsigned int |
| char | size_t | unsigned long |
| double | string | word |

For a demo, we create a project for the Arduino Nano 33 IoT. Open the Arduino software and write these codes.

```
void setup() {
  int a = 10;
  int b = 5;
```

```
// initialize serial communication
Serial.begin(115200);
while (!Serial) {
  ;
}

int c = a + b;
int d = a * b;

// print
Serial.print("C= ");
Serial.println(c);

Serial.print("d= ");
Serial.println(d);
}
void loop() {
}
```

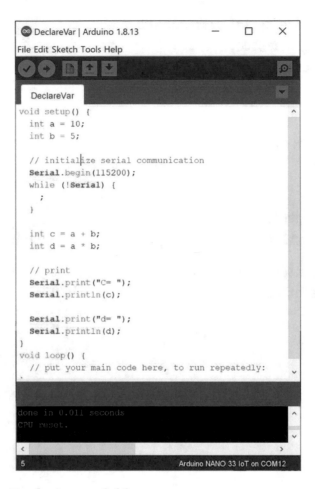

***Figure 2-1.***  *Declaring variables*

Figure 2-1 shows the aforementioned codes. To print messages, we use the Serial.print() and Serial.println() functions. We can print messages using Serial.print() without carriage return ("\r\n"). Otherwise, we can print messages with carriage return using Serial. println().

All printed messages with Serial library will be shown on the serial communication channel. Now we can save this program. Then, compile and upload to the Arduino Nano 33 IoT board.

To see the program output on the serial communication channel, we can use the Serial Monitor tool from Arduino. You can find it on the menu Tools ➤ Serial Monitor, as shown in Figure 2-2.

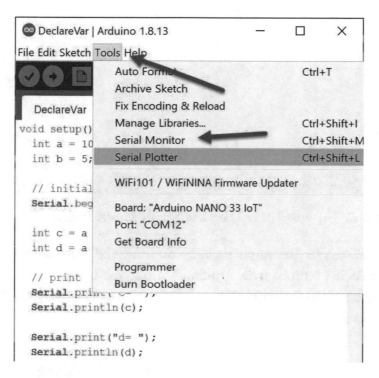

**Figure 2-2.**  *Opening the Serial Monitor tool*

After clicking the Serial Monitor tool, we can see our program output. Select baudrate 115200 on the bottom of the Serial Monitor tool. You should see the program output in Serial Monitor. Figure 2-3 shows my program output in the Serial Monitor tool.

```
COM12                                                    —    □    ×
|                                                                 Send
C= 15
d= 50




Autoscroll  Show timestamp         Both NL & CR  ∨  115200 baud  ∨  Clear output
```

*Figure 2-3.*  *Program output on the Serial Monitor tool*

If you don't see the output message on the Serial Monitor tool, you can click the RESET button on the Arduino Nano 33 IoT board. You can find this button next to the micro USB connector. You can see the RESET button position in Figure 2-4.

*Figure 2-4.*  *Clicking the RESET button on the Arduino Nano 33 IoT*

How does it work?

This program only runs on the setup() function. We declare two variables, a and b. Then, we assign their values.

```
void setup() {
  int a = 10;
  int b = 5;
```

Next, we activate the Serial object to perform serial communication. We set baud rate at 115200. We use while looping syntax to wait on creating Serial object.

```
// initialize serial communication
  Serial.begin(115200);
  while (!Serial) {
    ;
  }
```

We perform simple mathematic operations such as addition and multiplication. The result of the operations is stored in the c and d variables.

```
  int c = a + b;
  int d = a * b;
```

We print the result to serial terminal using the Serial object.

```
// print
Serial.print("C= ");
Serial.println(c);

Serial.print("d= ");
Serial.println(d);
```

On the `loop()` function, we do nothing. All codes run on the `setup()` function. That's why you probably don't see the program output, because we see it late.

```
void loop() {
}
```

# Operators

The Sketch program adopts C++ operators. We can declare arithmetic operators to perform mathematic operations. We can use the following arithmetic operators:

- % (remainder)

- * (multiplication)

- + (addition)

- - (subtraction)

- / (division)

- = (assignment operator)

For Boolean operators, we implement && for logical, || for logical or, and ! for logical not.

# Conditional Statement

We can perform action-based conditions. For instance, we want to turn on a lamp if a light sensor obtains a low intensity value. In Sketch, we implement a conditional statement using if and switch syntax. A conditional statement with if can be declared as follows:

```
if(<conditional>) {
// do something
} else {
// do something
}
```

We can put a conditional value on <conditional> such as applying Boolean and arithmetic operators. For a demo, we can create a Sketch program on the Arduino Nano 33 IoT. You write this complete program.

```
long num_a;
long num_b;

void setup() {
   // initialize serial communication
  Serial.begin(115200);
  while (!Serial) {
    ;
  }
}

void loop() {
  num_a = random(100);
  num_b = random(100);

  // print
  Serial.print("num_a: ");
  Serial.print(num_a);
  Serial.print(", num_b: ");
  Serial.println(num_b);
```

```
if(num_a > num_b) {
   Serial.println("num_a > num_b");
}else {
   Serial.println("num_a <= num_b");
}

delay(2000);
}
```

Save this program as conditional. Now you can compile and upload this program into the Arduino Nano 33 IoT board. Open the Serial Monitor tool so you can see this program output. Figure 2-5 shows my program output for a conditional program.

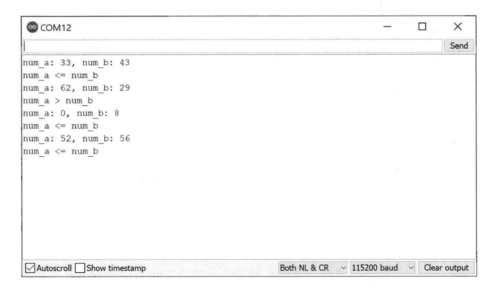

*Figure 2-5.* *Program output for a conditional if program*

How does this work?

This program generates random values for num_a and num_b variables on the loop() function.

```
void loop() {
  num_a = random(100);
  num_b = random(100);
```

Next, we print these random values on the serial terminal using the Serial object. We can call the Serial.print() and Serial.println() functions.

```
// print
Serial.print("num_a: ");
Serial.print(num_a);
Serial.print(", num_b: ");
Serial.println(num_b);
```

Last, we evaluate a value on num_a and num_b using a conditional-if statement. We check if the num_a value is greater than num_b or not. Then, we print the result on the serial terminal.

```
if(num_a > num_b) {
    Serial.println("num_a > num_b");
}else {
  Serial.println("num_a <= num_b");
}
```

The next demo is to implement a conditional with switch statement. In general, we can declare a switch statement as follows.

```
switch(value) {
        case val1: <code>
                            break;
        case val2: <code>
```

```
                              break;
           case val3: <code>
                              break;
}
```

For the demo, we build a program to evaluate the num_a value with a switch statement. We set a random value with a maximum value of 5. Open Arduino software and write this complete program.

```
long num_a;

void setup() {
  // initialize serial communication
  Serial.begin(115200);
  while (!Serial) {
    ;
  }
}
void loop() {
  num_a = random(5);

  // print
  Serial.print("num_a: ");
  Serial.println(num_a);
  switch(num_a) {
    case 0:
            Serial.println("num_a value is 0");
            break;
    case 1:
            Serial.println("num_a value is 1");
            break;
    case 2:
            Serial.println("num_a value is 2");
            break;
```

```
        case 3:
                Serial.println("num_a value is 3");
                break;
        case 4:
                Serial.println("num_a value is 4");
                break;
    }
    delay(2000);
}
```

Save this program as ConditionalSwitch. You can compile and upload this program into Arduino Nano 33 IoT. To see the program output, and you can open the Serial Monitor tool. You can see my program output in Figure 2-6.

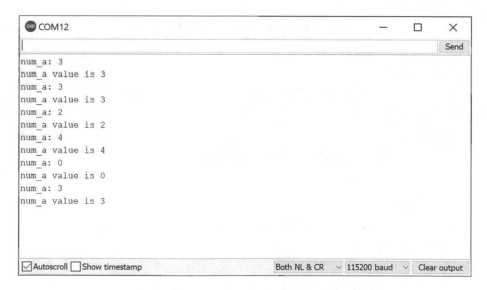

*Figure 2-6.* *Program output on the switch program*

How does this work?

This program starts to generate random values on the loop() function. The result is be stored in the num_a variable. Then, we print this value to a serial terminal.

```
void loop() {
  num_a = random(5);

  // print
  Serial.print("num_a: ");
  Serial.println(num_a);
```

Next, we evaluate the num_a variable using a switch statement. We check num_a for value: 0, 1, 2, 3, and 4. We print the message on each switch-case statement.

```
switch(num_a) {
    case 0:
            Serial.println("num_a value is 0");
            break;
    case 1:
            Serial.println("num_a value is 1");
            break;
    case 2:
            Serial.println("num_a value is 2");
            break;
    case 3:
            Serial.println("num_a value is 3");
            break;
    case 4:
            Serial.println("num_a value is 4");
            break;
  }
```

You have learned conditional statements with `if` and `switch`. In my opinion, you can use `switch` statements if the options are below 5; otherwise, you can use an `if`-statement with operators.

# Looping

The looping task is useful when you perform the same task continuously. In the Sketch program, we can implement looping tasks using `for`, `while`, and `do..while` statements. We can declare a for-statement as follows.

```
for(start;conditional;increment/decrement) {
         <codes>
}
```

For a while statement, we can implement as follows.

```
while(selection) {
         <codes>
}
```

We also can use `do..while` for looping. You can run the first code step, then we select a `while` statement.

```
do {
         <codes>
} while(selection);
```

Now we can build a Sketch program to implement looping using `for`, `while`, and `do..while` statement. Write this complete program using the Arduino software.

```
void setup() {
  // initialize serial communication
  Serial.begin(115200);
  while (!Serial) {
```

```
        ;
    }
}

void loop() {
    long val = random(15);
    int i;

    // print
    Serial.print("val: ");
    Serial.println(val);

    // looping
    Serial.println("Looping: for");
    for(i=0;i<val;i++){
        Serial.print(i);
        Serial.print(" ");
    }
    Serial.println();

    Serial.println("Looping: while");
    int start = 0;
    while(start < val) {
        Serial.print(start);
        Serial.print(" ");

        start++;
    }
    Serial.println();

    Serial.println("Looping: do..while");
    start = 0;
    do {
        Serial.print(start);
        Serial.print(" ");
```

```
    start++;
  }while(start < val);
  Serial.println();

  delay(3000);
}
```

You can save this program as Looping. You can compile and upload this program into the Arduino Nano 33 IoT board. After uploading a program into the Arduino Nano 33 IoT board, you can open the Serial Monitor tool to see program output. You can see my program output in Figure 2-7.

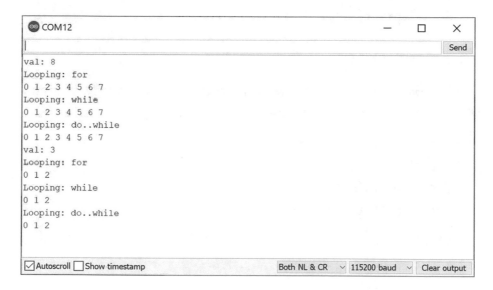

*Figure 2-7.* *Program output for looping*

How does it work?
We set a random value for our looping program.

```
void loop() {
  long val = random(15);
  int i;
```

We print this random value to serial terminal.

```
// print
Serial.print("val: ");
Serial.println(val);
```

For looping with a for statement, we perform a loop starting with i=0 until we reach val value.

```
Serial.println("Looping: for");
for(i=0;i<val;i++){
  Serial.print(i);
  Serial.print(" ");
}
Serial.println();
```

For a while statement, we perform a similar task to the for statement. We set start = 0 for initialization.

```
int start = 0;
while(start < val) {
  Serial.print(start);
  Serial.print(" ");

  start++;
}
Serial.println();
```

Last, we implement a do..while statement. We set start=0 again. Then, we perform a looping task.

```
start = 0;
  do {
    Serial.print(start);
    Serial.print(" ");
```

```
    start++;
  }while(start < val);
  Serial.println();
```

# Break and Continue

When we perform looping, we probably want to exit from looping or skip a certain step from looping. In the Sketch program, we can use break and continue statements.

For demo, we create the Sketch program to perform looping from 0 to a random value. When the looping iteration reaches 5, we skip this step using a continue statement. Then, we exit from looping when we reach an iteration value more than 10 using a break statement.

Now we can open Arduino software. We can write this complete program for break and continue implementation.

```
void setup() {
  // initialize serial communication
  Serial.begin(115200);
  while (!Serial) {
    ;
  }
}

void loop() {
  long val = random(6, 15);
  int i;

  // print
  Serial.print("val: ");
  Serial.println(val);
```

```
// looping
Serial.println("Looping: for");
for(i=0;i<val;i++){
  if(i==5)
    continue;

  if(i>10)
    break;

  Serial.print(i);
  Serial.print(" ");
}
Serial.println();

delay(3000);
}
```

Save this program as BreakContinue. Compile and upload this program into Arduino Nano 33 IoT. After uploading the program, we can see program output using the Serial Monitor tool, You can see my program output in Figure 2-8.

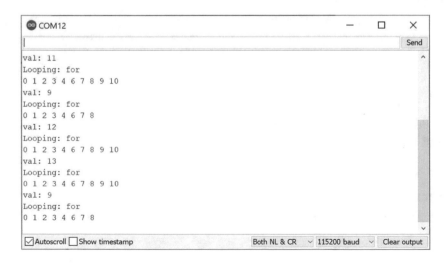

**Figure 2-8.** *Applying break and continue on the Sketch program*

How does it work?

We set a random value on the loop() function. We print this random value to the serial terminal using Serial object.

```
void loop() {
  long val = random(6, 15);
  int i;

  // print
  Serial.print("val: ");
  Serial.println(val);
```

We perform looping from 0 to a random value, val. When we have iteration = 5, we skip this iteration using the continue statement. Then, when we have iteration >10, we exit from looping by calling the break statement.

```
  // looping
  Serial.println("Looping: for");
  for(i=0;i<val;i++){
    if(i==5)
      continue;

    if(i>10)
      break;

    Serial.print(i);
    Serial.print(" ");
  }
  Serial.println();
```

This is the end of the basic Sketch program. Next, we write an Arduino program with various cases.

# Digital I/O

Arduino Nano 33 IoT has digital input/output about 14 pins. We can perform to attach sensors and actuators into digital I/O pins. You can see the Arduino Nano 33 IoT pin layout on the back of the board. Figure 2-9 shows the back of the Arduino Nano 33 IoT. Digital I/O pins are defined as Dx, where x is a digital number; for instance, D1 is digital I/O on pin 1.

***Figure 2-9.***  *Arduino Nano 33 IoT pinout*

To implement demo for digital I/O on the Arduino Nano 33 IoT, we need an LED and a push button. We will use internal LED (built-in LED) on digital pin 13. We also need a push button that is connected to digital pin 7. You can see our project wiring in Figure 2-10.

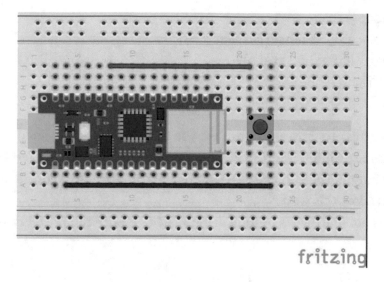

**Figure 2-10.** *A wiring for a push button project*

Now we create the Arduino program. In this program, we turn on the LED when the user clicks a push button. The program algorithm is to read a push button state using the digitalRead() function. To turn on the LED, we can use digitalWrite() and set HIGH value.

Open Arduino software. We can implement our program. Write this complete program.

```
int led = 13;
int pushButton = 7;
int state = 0;

void setup() {
  pinMode(led, OUTPUT);
  pinMode(pushButton, INPUT);
}
```

```
void loop() {
  state = digitalRead(pushButton);
  digitalWrite(led,state);
  delay(300);
}
```

Save this program as ButtonLed. You can compile and upload this program to Arduino Nano 33 IoT. After uploading, you can test by clicking a push button. You should see a lighting LED on Arduino Nano 33 IoT.

How does this work?

This program starts by initializing values for LED and push button pins.

```
int led = 13;
int pushButton = 7;
int state = 0;

void setup() {
  pinMode(led, OUTPUT);
  pinMode(pushButton, INPUT);
}
```

Then, on the loop() function, we read a push button state using the digitalRead() function. The state value will be passed to the digitalWrite() function to turn on/off LED.

```
void loop() {
  state = digitalRead(pushButton);
  digitalWrite(led,state);
  delay(300);
}
```

Now that we have learned about digital I/O, we will learn analog I/O in the next section.

# Analog I/O

Arduino Nano 33 IoT provides analog I/O to enable us to make interaction with sensor and actuator devices. We can see analog I/O pins with labeling Ax, where x is analog pin number. You can see these labels on the back of Arduino Nano 33 IoT.

You can see these pins in Figure 2-9. Arduino Nano 33 IoT has eight analog inputs (ADCs) and one analog input (DAC). For ADC model, Arduino Nano 33 IoT provides ADC resolution with 8-, 10-, and 12-bit. Furthermore, DAC model has a 10-bit resolution.

For our demo, we use the analog sensor TMP36. It's a temperature sensor. You can also use TMP36 module like thermal module from Linksprite, `https://www.linksprite.com/wiki/index.php?title=Thermal_Module`. You can perform wiring as shown in Figure 2-11. You can build this following wiring:

- TMP36 module VCC is connected to Arduino 3.3.V

- TMP36 module GND is connected to Arduino GND

- TMP36 module SIG is connected to Arduino analog A0

***Figure 2-11.*** *Wiring for analog sensor and Arduino Nano 33 IoT*

Now we can write an Arduino Program to analog sensor from TMP36 module. We read sensor data and then show it on a serial terminal. You can start by opening Arduino software and write this complete program.

```
void setup() {
  Serial.begin(115200);
  while (!Serial) {
    ;
  }
}

void loop() {
  int reading = analogRead(A0);

  float voltage = reading * 3.3;
  voltage /= 1024.0;

  Serial.print(voltage); Serial.println(" volts");

  float tempC = (voltage - 0.5) * 100 ;

  Serial.print(tempC);
  Serial.println(" degrees C");
  delay(3000);
}
```

Save this program as AnalogSensor. Now you can compile and upload this program into Arduino Nano 33 IoT. Open the Serial Monitor tool to see program output. Figure 2-12 shows my program output for the AnalogSensor program.

How does it work?

First, we read sensor data on analog pin A0.

```
void loop() {
  int reading = analogRead(A0);
```

Then, we calculate a voltage and show it on the serial terminal. Since we use a voltage reference of 3.3V, we can calculate using this formula:

```
float voltage = reading * 3.3;
voltage /= 1024.0;
```

```
Serial.print(voltage); Serial.println(" volts");
```

Now we can compute a temperate using the following formula-based datasheet from TMP36 module.

```
float tempC = (voltage - 0.5) * 100 ;
```

```
Serial.print(tempC);
Serial.println(" degrees C");
```

The result is be printed on serial terminal.

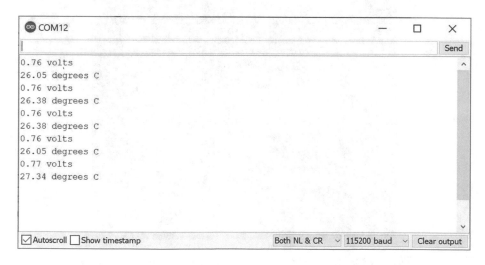

***Figure 2-12.*** *Program output for reading temperature*

# Plotting Analog Sensor

We also can plot analog input on the plotter tool. This tool is available on Arduino software. For our demo, we use a SparkFun Electret Microphone Breakout as an analog source. You can find this module on the link https://www.sparkfun.com/products/12758.

Now we can connect a SparkFun Electret Microphone Breakout to Arduino Nano 33 IoT. You can build this following the wiring:

- SparkFun Electret Microphone Breakout module VCC is connected to Arduino 3.3.V.

- SparkFun Electret Microphone Breakout module GND is connected to Arduino GND.

- SparkFun Electret Microphone Breakout module SIG is connected to Arduino A0.

You can see my hardware wiring in Figure 2-13.

***Figure 2-13.*** *Arduino wiring with SparkFun Electret Microphone Breakout*

Now we can write Arduino program to plot sensor data. Open Arduino software and write this complete program.

```
void setup() {
  Serial.begin(115200);
  while (!Serial) {
    ;
  }
}

void loop() {
  int val = analogRead(A0);
  Serial.println(val);
  delay(300);
}
```

Save this program as AnalogPlottIng. Now you can compile and upload this program into Arduino Nano 33 IoT. Open the Serial Plotter tool on Arduino software, and click the menu Tools ➤ Serial Plotter, as shown in Figure 2-14.

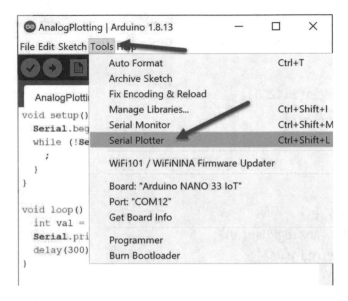

*Figure 2-14.*  *Opening the Serial Plotter tool*

After you click the Serial Plotter, you will obtain a dialog as shown in Figure 2-15. Make noise on SparkFun Electret Microphone Breakout so we can obtain various signals on the plotter tool. Since we use delay(300), plotter updates its graphs every 300 ms.

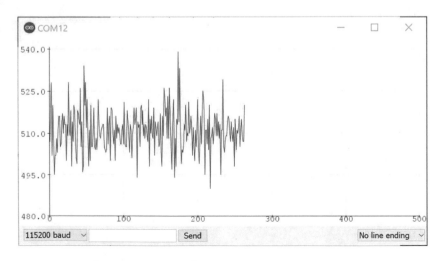

*Figure 2-15.*  *Plotting sensor data*

How does it work?

This program works very simply. First, we read an analog sensor by calling analogRead().

```
void loop() {
  int val = analogRead(A0);
```

Then, we print to the serial terminal using println() from the Serial object.

```
Serial.println(val);
delay(300);
```

This makes the Serial Plotter tool display a graph.

# Serial Communication

Serial communication is the process of sending data one bit at a time, sequentially, over a communication channel. In Arduino Nano 33 IoT, we can implement serial communication using the Serial object. We already used this Serial object in previous projects to show program output using the Serial Monitor tool.

We can write data into serial communication by calling print() and println() from Serial object. Further information about the Serial object, you can read it at https://www.arduino.cc/reference/en/ language/functions/communication/serial/.

For the demo, we build a blink program. Each LED state is written into a serial terminal. We use baudrate 115200. You can open Arduino software and write this complete program.

```
int led = 13;

void setup() {
  Serial.begin(115200);
  pinMode(led, OUTPUT);
}

void loop() {
  Serial.println("LED: HIGH");
  digitalWrite(led, HIGH);
  delay(1000);
  Serial.println("LED: LOW");
  digitalWrite(led, LOW);
  delay(1000);
}
```

Save this program as SerialDemo. Now you can compile and upload this program into Arduino Nano 33 IoT. Open the Serial Monitor tool to see the program output. Figure 2-16 shows my program output for the SerialDemo program.

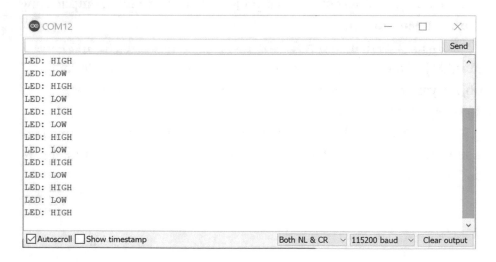

***Figure 2-16.*** *Program output for the SerialDemo program*

# Pulse Width Modulation

Pulse width modulation (PWM) is a method to control analog output. Technically, it's not "true" analog output. A microcontroller unit (MCU) can manipulate duty cycles to generate pulses. Arduino Nano 33 IoT has a PWM pin on digital pins. You can see a sign "~" on digital pins as a PWM pin. You can see that Figure 2-9 shows a digital pin such as D2 ~. In general, Arduino Nano 33 IoT has 11 PWM pins on 2, 3, 5, 6, 9, 10, 11, 12, 16/A2, 17/A3, and 19/A5.

For our demo, we use RGB LED. This LED has four pins. Three pins are red, green, and blue pins. The rest could be ground (GND) or voltage common collector (VCC), depending on RGB cathode or anode model.

We can implement our demo wiring as shown in Figure 2-17. You can perform the wiring as follows:

- RGB red pin is connected to Arduino digital pin 12.

- RGB green pin is connected to Arduino digital pin 11.

- RGB blue pin is connected to Arduino digital pin 10.

- RGB GND pin is connected to Arduino digital pin GND.

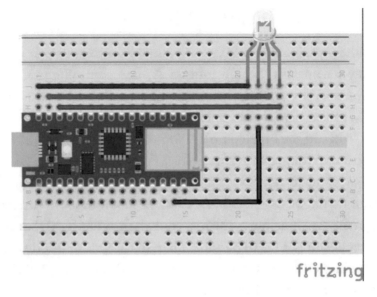

***Figure 2-17.*** *Wiring for Arduino and RGB LED*

Now we create the Arduino program to generate some colors with RGB LED. We will make colors such as red, green, blue, yellow, purple, and aqua. You can open Arduino software and write this complete program.

```
int redPin = 12;
int greenPin = 11;
int bluePin = 10;

void setup()
{
    pinMode(redPin, OUTPUT);
    pinMode(greenPin, OUTPUT);
    pinMode(bluePin, OUTPUT);
    Serial.begin(115200);
}
```

```
void loop()
{
  setColor(255, 0, 0);  // red
  Serial.println("red");
  delay(1000);
  setColor(0, 255, 0);  // green
  Serial.println("green");
  delay(1000);
  setColor(0, 0, 255);  // blue
  Serial.println("blue");
  delay(1000);
  setColor(255, 255, 0);  // yellow
  Serial.println("yellow");
  delay(1000);
  setColor(80, 0, 80);  // purple
  Serial.println("purple");
  delay(1000);
  setColor(0, 255, 255);  // aqua
  Serial.println("aqua");
  delay(1000);
}

void setColor(int red, int green, int blue)
{
  analogWrite(redPin, red);
  analogWrite(greenPin, green);
  analogWrite(bluePin, blue);
}
```

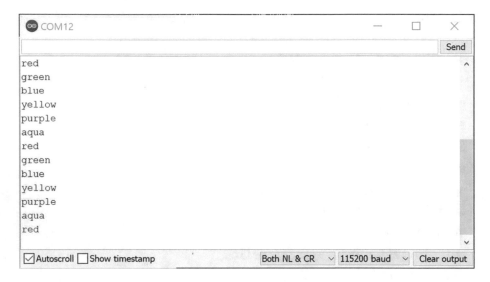

*Figure 2-18.* *Program output for the RGB application*

Save this program as test_rgb_arduino. Now you can compile and upload this program into Arduino Nano 33 IoT. You should see some colors on RGB LED. You also can open the Serial Monitor tool to see the program output. Figure 2-18 shows my program output for the test_rgb_arduino program.

How does it work?

We initialize digital pins for PWM pins. We call pinMode() with OUTPUT mode. We also configure serial with baudrate 115200.

```
int redPin = 12;
int greenPin = 11;
int bluePin = 10;

void setup()
{
    pinMode(redPin, OUTPUT);
    pinMode(greenPin, OUTPUT);
```

```
  pinMode(bluePin, OUTPUT);
  Serial.begin(115200);
}
```

We also define the setColor() function to generate a color from combining red, green, and blue color values. We call analogWrite() to write data for PWM data.

```
void setColor(int red, int green, int blue)
{
  analogWrite(redPin, red);
  analogWrite(greenPin, green);
  analogWrite(bluePin, blue);
}
```

Next, we generate some colors on the loop() function. For instance, we want to set red = 255, green = 0, and blue = 0. These sample for generating colors for red, green, and blue.

```
void loop()
{
  setColor(255, 0, 0);  // red
  Serial.println("red");
  delay(1000);
  setColor(0, 255, 0);  // green
  Serial.println("green");
  delay(1000);
  setColor(0, 0, 255);  // blue
  Serial.println("blue");
  delay(1000);
```

We also generate colors for yellow, purple, and aqua by inserting values for red, green, and blue.

```
setColor(255, 255, 0);  // yellow
Serial.println("yellow");
delay(1000);
setColor(80, 0, 80);  // purple
Serial.println("purple");
delay(1000);
setColor(0, 255, 255);  // aqua
Serial.println("aqua");
delay(1000);
```

You can practice generating new colors by combining values for red, green, and blue. We can only set values from 0 to 255.

# Serial Peripheral Interface

Serial communication works with asynchronous mode so there is no control on serial communication. This means we cannot guarantee the data that is sent will be received by receiver. The serial peripheral interface (SPI) is a synchronous serial communication interface specification, but SPI has four wires to control data such as master out/slave in (MOSI), master in/slave out (MISO), serial clock signal (SCLK), and slave select (SS).

Arduino Nano 33 IoT has one SPI interface with the following SPI pins:

- MOSI on Digital pin 11

- MISO on Digital pin 12

- SCLK on Digital pin 13

You can attach any sensor or actuator-based SPI interface on Arduino Nano 33 IoT. For our demo, we only connect the MISO pin to the MOSI pin using a jumper cable. You can connect digital pin 12 to digital pin 11. Figure 2-19 shows my wiring for the SPI demo.

***Figure 2-19.***  *Connecting MISO and MISO pins from Arduino SPI*

To access the SPI interface on Arudino Nano 33 IoT, we can use the SPI library. You can obtain a detailed information about this library at this link, https://www.arduino.cc/en/Reference/SPI.

Now we can build the Arduino program. Our program will send data to SPI and receive data from SPI. Open Arduino software and then write this complete program.

```
#include <SPI.h>

byte sendData,recvData;
void setup() {
  SPI.begin();
```

```
  Serial.begin(9600);
  randomSeed(80);
}
void loop() {
  sendData = random(50, 100);
  recvData = SPI.transfer(sendData);

  Serial.print("Send=");
  Serial.println(sendData,DEC);
  Serial.print("Recv=");
  Serial.println(recvData,DEC);
  delay(800);
}
```

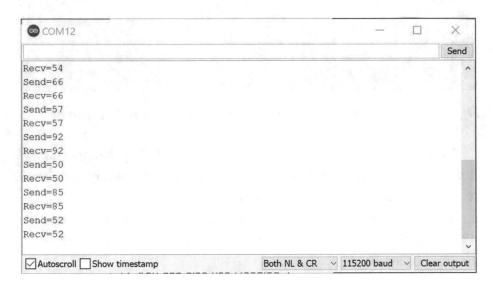

***Figure 2-20.*** *Program output for the SPI program*

Save this program as SPIDemo. Now you can compile and upload
this program into Arduino Nano 33 IoT. You can open the Serial Monitor
tool to see program output. Figure 2-20 shows my program output for the
SPIDemo program.

How does it work?

We initialize SPI and Serial interface on the setup() function.

```
#include <SPI.h>

byte sendData,recvData;
void setup() {
  SPI.begin();
  Serial.begin(9600);
  randomSeed(80);
}
```

To send and receive data over SPI, we can use the SPI.transfer() function. We send data with a random value on the loop() function.

```
void loop() {
  sendData = random(50, 100);
  recvData = SPI.transfer(sendData);
```

Then, we print sent data and received data on serial terminal.

```
Serial.print("Send=");
Serial.println(sendData,DEC);
Serial.print("Recv=");
Serial.println(recvData,DEC);
```

You have completed the SPI demo. You can practice more with SPI by applying sensors or actuator devices.

# Interintegrated Circuit (I2C)

The interintegrated circuit (I2C) protocol is a protocol intended to allow multiple "slave" module/device (chip) to communicate with one or more "master" chips. This protocol works with asynchronous mode.

To communicate with other devices/modules, I2C protocol defines the I2C address for all "slave" devices.

The I2C interface has two pins: serial data (SDA) and serial clock (SCL). For data transfer, the I2C interface uses an SDA pin. An SCL pin is used for clocking. The Arduino Nano 33 IoT board has I2C pins on A4 as SDA and A5 as SCL.

For our demo, we use a sensor module-based I2C interface. The I2C interface uses a device address so the Arduino Nano 33 IoT board can access data by opening a connection to the I2C address. Each analog sensor from sensor module-based I2C will be attached to the I2C address.

For testing, I used a PCF8591 AD/DA converter module with sensor and actuator devices. This sensor module can be seen in Figure 2-21. The PCF8591 AD/DA module uses a PCF8591 chip that consists of four analog input and AD converters. The PCF8591 chip also has analog output with a DA converter. For further information about the PCF8591 chip, you can read at this link, `https://www.nxp.com/products/interfaces/ic-spi-serial-interface-devices/ic-dacs-and-adcs/8-bit-a-d-and-d-a-converter:PCF8591`.

You can find the chip at an online store like Aliexpress. You can probably obtain this module at your local store.

***Figure 2-21.*** *PCF8591 ADC DAC AD/DA module*

Based on datasheet documentation of the PCF8591 AD/DA converter module, this module uses I2C addresses on 0x48. The PCF8591 AD/DA converter module also consists of three sensors as follows:

- Thermistor: using channel 0

- Photoresistor: using channel 1

- Potentiometer: using channel 3

Now attach the PCF8591 AD/DA converter module to the Arduino Nano 33 IoT board with the following wiring:

- The PCF8591 AD/DA module SDA is connected to Arduino A4 pin.

- The PCF8591 AD/DA module SCL is connected to Arduino A5 pin.

- The PCF8591 AD/DA module VCC is connected to Arduino 3.3V.

- The PCF8591 AD/DA module GND is connected to Arduino GND pin.

Figure 2-22 shows my wiring for the PCF8591 AD/DA converter module and Arduino Nano 33 IoT. You should see a lighting LED when we plug in 3.3V to the module.

***Figure 2-22.*** *Wiring PCF8591 ADC DAC AD/DA module with Arduino Nano 33 IoT*

We have finished our wiring for this demo. Next, we will implement two project demos as listed here:

- I2C scanning application

- I2C sensor application

Next, we build a scanning I2C address application on the Arduino Nano 33 IoT board.

## Scanning I2C Address

Every device/module-based I2C set owns an I2C address on MCU. In this section, we want to scan all devices that are attached on Arduino Nano 33 IoT. We also have two internal sensor device-based I2Cs inside Arduino Nano 33 IoT.

To access I2C on the Arduino board, we can use the Wire library. We can include our program by inserting the wire.h library. For further information about the Wire library, we can read on the official website from Arduino (https://www.arduino.cc/en/Reference/Wire).

For our demo, we use our wiring demo from the PCF8591 AD/DA converter module (see Figure 2-22). Open Arduino software and write this complete program.

```
#include <Wire.h>

void setup() {

  Serial.begin(115200);
  Wire.begin();
  Serial.println("\nI2C Scanner");
}

void loop() {
  byte error, address;
  int nDevices;

  Serial.println("Scanning...");

  nDevices = 0;
  for(address = 1; address < 127; address++) {
    Wire.beginTransmission(address);
    error = Wire.endTransmission();

    if (error == 0) {
      Serial.print("I2C device found at address 0x");
      if (address < 16)
        Serial.print("0");
      Serial.println(address, HEX);

      nDevices++;
    }
```

```
    else if (error == 4) {
      Serial.print("Unknown error at address 0x");
      if (address < 16)
        Serial.print("0");
      Serial.println(address, HEX);
    }
  }
  if (nDevices == 0)
    Serial.println("No I2C devices found");
  else
    Serial.println("done");

  delay(5000);
}
```

Save this program as i2c_scanner. Now you can compile and upload this program into Arduino Nano 33 IoT. We can see program output using Serial Monitor.

Figure 2-23 shows my program output for i2c_scanner. You can see that there are three I2C addresses. 0x48 is our PCF8591 AD/DA converter module. Two I2C addresses, 0x60 and 0x6A, are internal I2C sensors inside Arduino Nano 33 IoT.

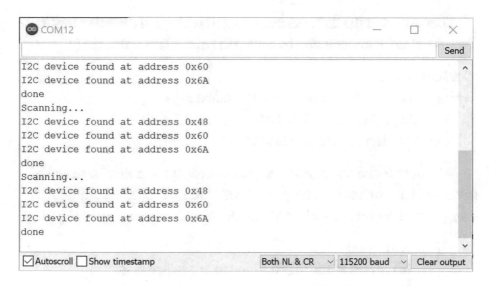

**Figure 2-23.** *Program output for reading I2C address*

How does it work?

First, we initialize I2C and serial interfaces on the setup() function. We set baudrate serial for 115200.

```
#include <Wire.h>

void setup() {

  Serial.begin(115200);
  Wire.begin();
  Serial.println("\nI2C Scanner");
}
```

On the loop() function, we scan the I2C address by probing I2C data. We set initialize nDevices = 0 for a number of finding I2C devices. We perform a looping task from address 0 to 127.

Then we open the I2C interface using `Wire.beginTransmission()`. Next, we close a transmission by calling `wire.endTransmission()`.

```
nDevices = 0;
  for(address = 1; address < 127; address++) {
    Wire.beginTransmission(address);
    error = Wire.endTransmission();
```

We check for value error. If there is no error, it means we have an I2C device on current address. We print the I2C address to serial terminal using `Serial.println()` with HEX mode.

```
    if (error == 0) {
      Serial.print("I2C device found at address 0x");
      if (address < 16)
        Serial.print("0");
      Serial.println(address, HEX);

      nDevices++;
    }
```

Otherwise, we check the error code. If error = 4, we print errors on this address for unknown errors on the current address.

```
    else if (error == 4) {
      Serial.print("Unknown error at address 0x");
      if (address < 16)
        Serial.print("0");
      Serial.println(address, HEX);
    }
```

Last, we print our findings from the I2C interface on the serial terminal.

```
if (nDevices == 0)
  Serial.println("No I2C devices found");
else
  Serial.println("done");
```

This program is useful to check a list of I2C devices that are attached on Arduino Nano 33 IoT.

# Reading Sensor-Based I2C Address

In this section, we read sensor data from the I2C device. We already configured hardware wiring in Figure 2-22. The PCF8591 AD/DA converter module has three sensors: thermistor, photo-voltaic cell, and potentiometer. Each sensor has a channel address on 0x00, 0x01, and 0x03, respectively.

Let's start to build the Arduino program to access sensor device over the I2C interface. We will use hardware wiring in Figure 2-22. You can open the Arduino software and write this complete program.

```
#include "Wire.h"
#define PCF8591 0x48 // I2C bus address
#define PCF8591_ADC_CH0 0x00 // thermistor
#define PCF8591_ADC_CH1 0x01 // photo-voltaic cell
#define PCF8591_ADC_CH2 0x02
#define PCF8591_ADC_CH3 0x03 // potentiometer
byte ADC1, ADC2, ADC3;

void setup()
{
  Wire.begin();
  Serial.begin(9600);
```

```
}
void loop()
{
  // read thermistor
  Wire.beginTransmission(PCF8591);
  Wire.write((byte)PCF8591_ADC_CH0);
  Wire.endTransmission();
  delay(100);
  Wire.requestFrom(PCF8591, 2);
  delay(100);
  ADC1=Wire.read();
  ADC1=Wire.read();

  Serial.print("Thermistor=");
  Serial.println(ADC1);

  // read photo-voltaic cell
  Wire.beginTransmission(PCF8591);
  Wire.write(PCF8591_ADC_CH1);
  Wire.endTransmission();
  delay(100);
  Wire.requestFrom(PCF8591, 2);
  delay(100);
  ADC2=Wire.read();
  ADC2=Wire.read();

  Serial.print("Photo-voltaic cell=");
  Serial.println(ADC2);

  // potentiometer
  Wire.beginTransmission(PCF8591);
  Wire.write(PCF8591_ADC_CH3);
  Wire.endTransmission();
```

```
delay(100);
Wire.requestFrom(PCF8591, 2);
delay(100);
ADC3=Wire.read();
ADC3=Wire.read();

Serial.print("potentiometer=");
Serial.println(ADC3);

delay(500);
}
```

Save this program as I2CSensor. Now you can compile and upload this program into Arduino Nano 33 IoT. Open the Serial Monitor tool on Arduino software. You should see sensor data from the I2C protocol. Figure 2-24 shows my program output for the I2CSensor.

***Figure 2-24.*** *Program output for reading sensors over I2C*

How does it work?

First, we initialize our I2C, Serial, and PCF8591 AD/DA converter module. We define I2C address channel. This is done on the setup() function.

```
#include "Wire.h"
#define PCF8591 0x48 // I2C bus address
#define PCF8591_ADC_CH0 0x00 // thermistor
#define PCF8591_ADC_CH1 0x01 // photo-voltaic cell
#define PCF8591_ADC_CH2 0x02
#define PCF8591_ADC_CH3 0x03 // potentiometer
byte ADC1, ADC2, ADC3;

void setup()
{
  Wire.begin();
  Serial.begin(9600);
}
```

We can read sensor data on the loop() function. To read thermistor data, we open I2C using Wire.beginTransmission() with passing PCF8591. Then, select a channel for thermistor with value PCF8591_ADC_CH0 using Wire.write(). We close transmission by calling Wire.endTransmission(). We read sensor data with 2 bytes using the Wire.requestFrom() function.

```
void loop()
{
  // read thermistor
  Wire.beginTransmission(PCF8591);
  Wire.write((byte)PCF8591_ADC_CH0);
  Wire.endTransmission();
  delay(100);
```

```
Wire.requestFrom(PCF8591, 2);
delay(100);
ADC1=Wire.read();
ADC1=Wire.read();
```

We set delay(100) to wait the module to complete our request. We read a data per byte using the Wire.read() function. Next, we print thermistor data on the serial terminal.

```
Serial.print("Thermistor=");
Serial.println(ADC1);
```

With the same method, we can read photo-voltaic cell by changing channel the value PCF8591_ADC_CH1. After that, we read sensor data and print the result to the serial terminal.

```
// read photo-voltaic cell
Wire.beginTransmission(PCF8591);
Wire.write(PCF8591_ADC_CH1);
Wire.endTransmission();
delay(100);
Wire.requestFrom(PCF8591, 2);
delay(100);
ADC2=Wire.read();
ADC2=Wire.read();
```

```
Serial.print("Photo-voltaic cell=");
Serial.println(ADC2);
```

We also read potentiometer from the PCF8591 AD/DA converter module. Open the I2C interface and select the channel for PCF8591_ADC_ CH3. Then, we can read sensor data and print it on the serial terminal.

```
// potentiometer
Wire.beginTransmission(PCF8591);
Wire.write(PCF8591_ADC_CH3);
Wire.endTransmission();
delay(100);
Wire.requestFrom(PCF8591, 2);
delay(100);
ADC3=Wire.read();
ADC3=Wire.read();

Serial.print("potentiometer=");
Serial.println(ADC3);
```

This is the end of the chapter. You can practice more on Arduino Nano 33 IoT with some protocol that we already learned.

# Summary

We have learned basic Arduino programming using Sketch. We accessed digital and analog I/O on the Arduino Nano 33 IoT board. We explored how to implement PWM on Arduino Nano 33 IoT and how to plot sensor data. Furthermore, we learned to use SPI and I2C interfaces to communicate with external devices.

Next, we will learn how to access internal sensor devices on Arduino Nano 33 IoT.

# CHAPTER 3

# IMU Sensor: Accelerator and Gyroscope

The Arduino Nano 33 IoT board has an internal sensor, inertial measurement unit (IMU). This IMU sensor is built from LSM6DS3. In this chapter, we explore how to access the IMU sensor on Arduino Nano 33 IoT.

You will learn the following topics in this chapter:

- Setting up LSM6DS3 sensor

- Accessing accelerator sensor

- Accessing gyroscope sensor

- Plotting sensor data

## Introduction

Arduino Nano 33 IoT has an internal sensor that we can access directly. This sensor is the IMU-based LSM6DS3. This module consists of accelerator and gyroscope sensors. This sensor is connected to Arduino Nano 33 IoT over the interintegrated circuit (I2C) interface. For further

© Agus Kurniawan 2021
A. Kurniawan, *Beginning Arduino Nano 33 IoT*,
https://doi.org/10.1007/978-1-4842-6446-1_3

information about technical documentation of LSM6DS3, we can read the detailed datasheet document at this link, `https://content.arduino.cc/ assets/st_imu_lsm6ds3_datasheet.pdf`. You can see the LSM6DS3 chip on Arduino Nano 33 IoT board in Figure 3-1.

***Figure 3-1.*** *LSM6DS3 chip on Arduino Nano 33 IoT*

In Chapter 2, we learned about the I2C interface. We also perform a scan of the I2C address. You can run the i2c_scanner program from Chapter 2. Figure 3-2 shows a list of I2C addresses of I2C devices. The IMU sensor runs on 0x60 and x6A I2C addresses.

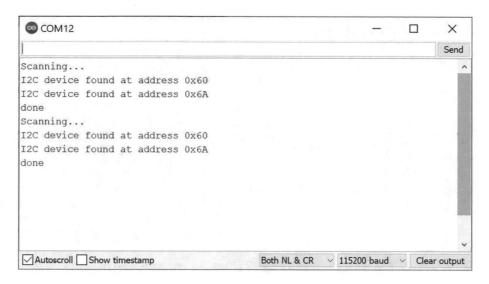

***Figure 3-2.*** *A list I2C addresses from sensor device-based I2C interface*

In this chapter, we will explore the IMU sensor, LSM6DS3, on Arduino Nano 33 IoT. We access accelerator and gyroscope sensors from the Arduino program.

# Set Up LSM6DS3 Library

To access the IMU sensor-based LSM6DS3 chip on Arduino Nano 33 IoT, we need to install the Arduino LSM6DS3 library. This library can be used to access the IMU sensor for accelerator and gyroscope sensors. We will use this library in this chapter. Details about the LSM6DS3 library can be read at this link, `https://www.arduino.cc/en/Reference/ArduinoLSM6DS3`.

To install the Arduino LSM6DS3 library, you can open Arduino software. Then, click the menu Sketch ➤ Include Library ➤ Manage Libraries, as shown in Figure 3-3.

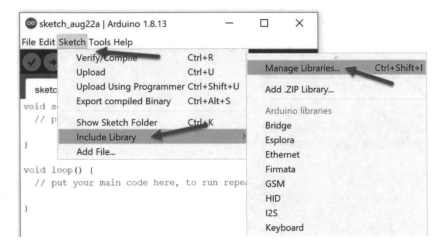

***Figure 3-3.*** *Opening the Manage Libraries menu in Arduino software*

After we click the Manage Libraries menu, we will obtain a Library Manager dialog, as shown in Figure 3-4. You can type **arduino_lsm6ds3** in the search textbox. Then, you should see a list of libraries. You should also see the Arduino_LSM6DS3 library. In Figure 3-4 you can see the Arduino_ LSM6DS3 library that is noted by a red arrow.

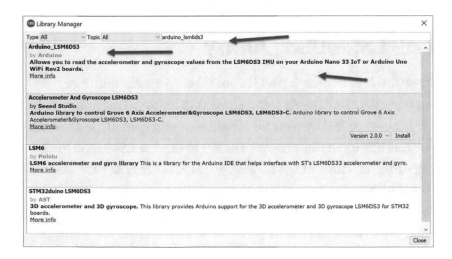

***Figure 3-4.*** *Installing the Arduino LSM6DS3 library*

Click the Install button after you click the Arduino_LSM6DS3 library. Make sure your computer is connected to the Internet. After completing installation, we can access the IMU sensor on Arduino Nano 33 IoT.

# Working with an Accelerator

The IMU sensor in Arduino Nano 33 IoT has an accelerator sensor. This sensor measures acceleration on x, y, and z coordinates. The sensor value ranges from -4 to 4. We will use the Arduino LSM6DS6 library to access the IMU accelerator sensor.

In general, we can start to use the LSM6DS6 library by calling IMU.begin(). Then, we can read the sensor value by calling the IMU. readAcceleration() function.

For the demo, we read the IMU accelerator on the Arduino Nano 33 IoT board. Then, we print the measurement result on the serial terminal. You can open Arduino software and write this complete program.

```
#include <Arduino_LSM6DS3.h>

void setup() {
  Serial.begin(115200);
  while (!Serial);

  if (!IMU.begin()) {
    Serial.println("Failed to initialize IMU!");

    while (1);
  }

  Serial.print("Accelerometer sample rate = ");
  Serial.print(IMU.accelerationSampleRate());
  Serial.println(" Hz");
  Serial.println();
```

```
  Serial.println("Acceleration in G's");
  Serial.println("X\tY\tZ");
}

void loop() {
  float x, y, z;

  if (IMU.accelerationAvailable()) {
    IMU.readAcceleration(x, y, z);

    Serial.print(x);
    Serial.print('\t');
    Serial.print(y);
    Serial.print('\t');
    Serial.println(z);
  }
}
```

Save this program as SimpleAccelerometer. Now you can compile and upload this program into Arduino Nano 33 IoT. We can see program output using the Serial Monitor. Change your board position or shake your board or move your board with certain speed so you have a measurement result on the serial terminal.

Figure 3-5 shows my program output for the SimpleAccelerometer program. You can see accelerator values for x, y, and z.

```
COM12                                          —    □    ×
                                                          Send
0.03      0.46      0.93                                      ^
0.02      0.36      0.96
-0.06     0.31      1.10
-0.05     0.24      1.16
0.05      0.18      1.03
0.05      0.15      1.02
0.08      0.18      0.88
-0.01     0.15      0.83
-0.03     0.14      0.84
-0.04     0.20      0.81
-0.06     0.46      0.71
-0.05     0.66      0.62
-0.06     0.72      0.58
                                                             v
☑Autoscroll ☐Show timestamp       Both NL & CR ∨ 115200 baud ∨  Clear output
```

**Figure 3-5.**  *Program output from reading the IMU accelerator*

How does it work?

First, we include the Arduino LSM6DS3 library in the Arduino program.

```
#include <Arduino_LSM6DS3.h>
```

We initialize the IMU sensor and the Serial object on the setup()
function.

```
void setup() {
  Serial.begin(115200);
  while (!Serial);

  if (!IMU.begin()) {
    Serial.println("Failed to initialize IMU!");

    while (1);
  }
```

We also can print the current accelerator sample rate by calling the
IMU.accelerationSampleRate() function on the serial terminal.

85

```
Serial.print("Accelerometer sample rate = ");
Serial.print(IMU.accelerationSampleRate());
Serial.println(" Hz");
Serial.println();
Serial.println("Acceleration in G's");
Serial.println("X\tY\tZ");
```

On the `loop()` function, we read the accelerator sensor. We should check whether there is available accelerator sensor data by calling the `IMU.accelerationAvailable()` function. If it's available for sensor data, we can read the sensor data using the `IMU.readAcceleration()` function.

```
void loop() {
  float x, y, z;

  if (IMU.accelerationAvailable()) {
    IMU.readAcceleration(x, y, z);
```

Then, we print the sensor data on the serial terminal.

```
    Serial.print(x);
    Serial.print('\t');
    Serial.print(y);
    Serial.print('\t');
    Serial.println(z);
```

# Working with Gyroscope

Gyroscope is a sensor to measure orientation and angular velocity. Arduino Nano 33 IoT has a built-in gyroscope sensor over the IMU LSM6DS3 sensor chip. We can access this sensor using the Arduino LSM6DS3 library.

For our demo, we read the gyroscope sensor using the Arduino LSM6DS3 library. Then, we print sensor data in the serial terminal. Open Arduino software and write this complete program.

```
#include <Arduino_LSM6DS3.h>

void setup() {
  Serial.begin(9600);
  while (!Serial);

  if (!IMU.begin()) {
    Serial.println("Failed to initialize IMU!");

    while (1);
  }

  Serial.print("Gyroscope sample rate = ");
  Serial.print(IMU.gyroscopeSampleRate());
  Serial.println(" Hz");
  Serial.println();
  Serial.println("Gyroscope in degrees/second");
  Serial.println("X\tY\tZ");
}

void loop() {
  float x, y, z;

  if (IMU.gyroscopeAvailable()) {
    IMU.readGyroscope(x, y, z);

    Serial.print(x);
    Serial.print('\t');
    Serial.print(y);
    Serial.print('\t');
    Serial.println(z);
  }
}
```

Save this program as SimpleGyroscope. Now you can compile and upload this program into Arduino Nano 33 IoT. We can see the program output using the Serial Monitor. Change your board orientation to see the change values on the Serial Monitor tool.

Figure 3-6 shows my program output for the SimpleGyroscope program. You can see gyroscope values for x, y, and z.

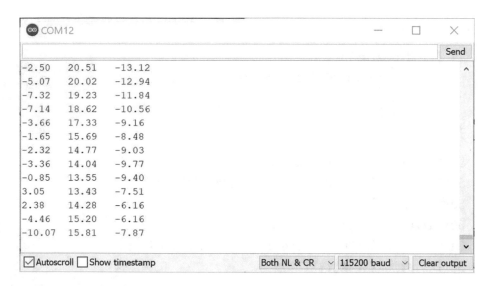

***Figure 3-6.*** *Program output from reading the gyroscope sensor*

How does it work?

First, we include the Arduino LSM6DS3 library in the Arduino program.

```
#include <Arduino_LSM6DS3.h>
```

We initialize the IMU sensor to enable work with the gyroscope sensor and the Serial object on the setup() function.

```
void setup() {
  Serial.begin(115200);
  while (!Serial);
```

```
if (!IMU.begin()) {
  Serial.println("Failed to initialize IMU!");

  while (1);
}
```

We also can print the current gyroscope sample rate by calling the IMU.gyroscopeSampleRate() function on the serial terminal.

```
Serial.print("Gyroscope sample rate = ");
Serial.print(IMU.gyroscopeSampleRate());
Serial.println(" Hz");
Serial.println();
Serial.println("Gyroscope in degrees/second");
Serial.println("X\tY\tZ");
```

On the loop() function, we read the gyroscope sensor. We should check whether there is available gyroscope sensor data by calling the IMU.gyroscopeAvailable() function. If it's available for the Gyroscope sensor data, we can read sensor data using the IMU.readGyroscope() function.

```
void loop() {
  float x, y, z;

  if (IMU.gyroscopeAvailable()) {
    IMU.readGyroscope(x, y, z);
```

Then, we print the sensor data on the serial terminal.

```
  Serial.print(x);
  Serial.print('\t');
  Serial.print(y);
  Serial.print('\t');
  Serial.println(z);
```

This is the end of the project. You can practice by applying the IMU sensor in your projects.

# Plotting Sensor Data

We can read sensor data from built-in sensor devices on Arduino Nano 33 IoT. In this section, we will plot our sensor using the Serial Plotter tool from Arduino. For testing, we will use previous projects that read the Gyroscope sensor.

You can open Arduino software. We initialize our Gyroscope sensor and serial communication on the setup() function. We set serial baudrate 115200 and initialize Gyroscope by calling the IMU.begin() function.

```
#include <Arduino_LSM6DS3.h>

void setup() {
  Serial.begin(115200);
  while (!Serial);

  if (!IMU.begin()) {
    Serial.println("Failed to initialize IMU!");

    while (1);
  }
}
```

On the loop() function, we read the Gyroscope sensor using IMU. readGyroscope(). First, we should check availability of sensor data by calling the IMU.gyroscopeAvailable() function. We store the Gyroscope sensor to x, y, and z variables.

```
void loop() {
  float x, y, z;

  if (IMU.gyroscopeAvailable()) {
    IMU.readGyroscope(x, y, z);
```

To plot the Gyroscope sensor to the Serial Plotter tool, we can print sensor values with the "," delimiter. For instance, we print x, y, and z sensor variables as follows.

```
    Serial.print(x);
    Serial.print(',');
    Serial.print(y);
    Serial.print(',');
    Serial.println(z);
  }
}
```

Now save this program as GyroscopePlotter program. Then, you can compile and upload this program in Arduino Nano 33 IoT.

After uploading the program, you can open the Serial Plotter from the Tools menu in Arduino software. You should see sensor outputs on the Serial Plotter too. Figure 3-7 shows my program output from the GyroscopePlotter program.

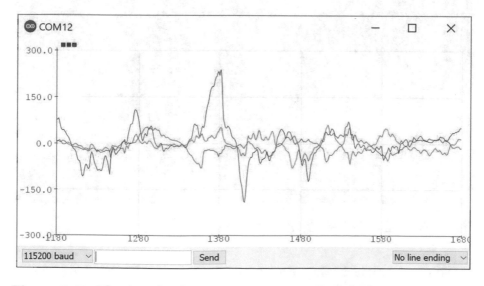

*Figure 3-7.* *Plotting the Gyroscope sensor on Serial Plotter*

# Displaying Sensor Data with Organic Light-Emitting Diode I2C Display

In this section, we want to display sensor data on an organic light-emitting diode (OLED) display. There are two interface models on OLED display: serial peripheral interface (SPI) and I2C. In this demo, we will use the OLED I2C display. You can buy any OLED I2C display module in a local electronic store. You can probably find it on Aliexpress or Alibaba.

For this demo, I use the OLED I2C display with 0.96 inch or 128 x 64 pixels. You can see my OLED I2C display in Figure 3-8.

***Figure 3-8.***  *OLED 0.96-inch I2C display*

You can use any display size for the OLED I2C display. Next, we will wire the OLED I2C display for Arduino Nano 33 IoT.

# Wiring for Arduino Nano 33 IoT and the OLED I2C Display

We use the OLED display with an I2C interface so we can connect this OLED display to Arduino Nano 33 IoT over I2C pins. You can see my wiring in Figure 3-9. You can perform this wiring as follows:

- The OLED I2C display module serial data is connected to the Arduino A4 pin.

- The OLED I2C display module serial clock is connected to the Arduino A5 pin.

- The OLED I2C display module voltage common collector (VCC) is connected to Arduino 3.3V.

- The OLED I2C display module ground (GND) is connected to the Arduino GND pin.

***Figure 3-9.*** *Wiring the OLED I2C display on Arduino Nano 33 IoT*

Next, we can build the Arduino program for the OLED I2C display.

## Checking the I2C Address of the OLED I2C Display

After we make wiring between the Arduino Nano 33 IoT and the OLED I2C display, we can use the i2c_scanner program from Chapter 2 to check the I2C address from devices. We want to know the I2C address from the OLED I2C display.

Load the i2c_scanner program into Arduino software. Then, compile and upload this program into Arduino Nano 33 IoT. After that, open the Serial Monitor tool. You should see three I2C addresses. Two of them are I2C built-in sensors on Arduino Nano 33 IoT. The rest is our OLED I2C display.

You can see my program output in Figure 3-10. You can see my OLED I2C display running on the 0x3C I2C address. Two I2C addresses, 0x60 and x6A, are I2C built-in sensors on Arduino Nano 33 IoT.

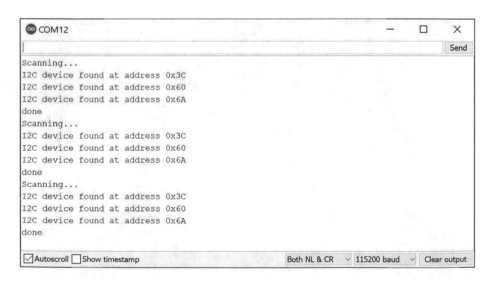

*Figure 3-10.* *Detecting I2C addresses for the OLED I2C display*

Next, we set up libraries in order to build programs for OLED I2C display on Arduino Nano 33 IoT.

# Setting up the OLED I2C Display Library

To work with the OLED I2C display on Arduino, we need to install two of the following libraries from Adafruit:

- Adafruit_SSD1306, `https://github.com/adafruit/Adafruit_SSD1306`

- Adafruit GFX Library, `https://github.com/adafruit/Adafruit-GFX-Library`

We can install these libraries via Library Manager on Arduino software. Type Adafruit_SSD1306 and Adafruit GFX Library to install these libraries. Figure 3-11 shows Adafruit_SSD1306 library.

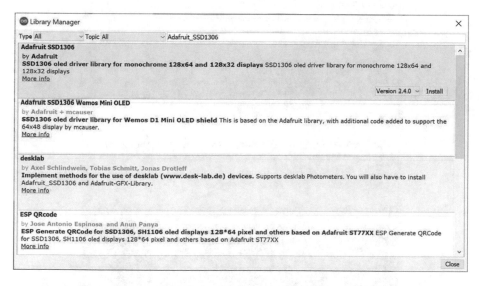

***Figure 3-11.*** *Adding libraries for the OLED I2C display*

Install these libraries. You will probably be asked to install additional libraries to enable work with Adafruit_SSD1306 and Adafruit GFX library—for instance, Adafruit BusIO.

# Testing the OLED I2C Display

After we installed the Adafruit_SSD1306 library, we can test our OLED I2C display. We can use program samples from Adafruit_SSD1306 library. You can find it in the menu File ➤ Examples ➤ Adafruit_SSD1306 ➤ ssd1306_128x64_i2c. After clicked, you should obtain codes as shown in Figure 3-12.

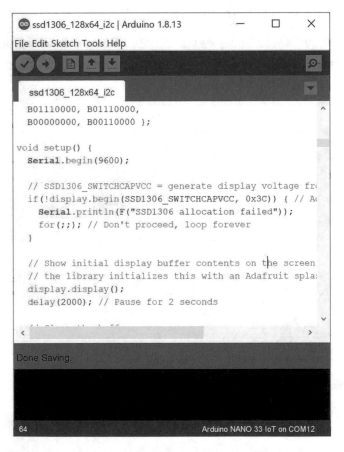

*Figure 3-12.* *A program sample for the OLED I2C display*

Next, we modify this program with the I2C address from our OLED I2C display. In the previous section, we had the 0x3C address for the OLED I2C display. Replace the I2C address `display.begin()` with 0x3C, as shown in Figure 3-12.

Now you can compile and upload this program to Arduino Nano 33 IoT. You should see some forms on the OLED I2C display. Figure 3-13 shows program output from ssd1306_128x64_i2c on the OLED I2C display with 128x64 pixels.

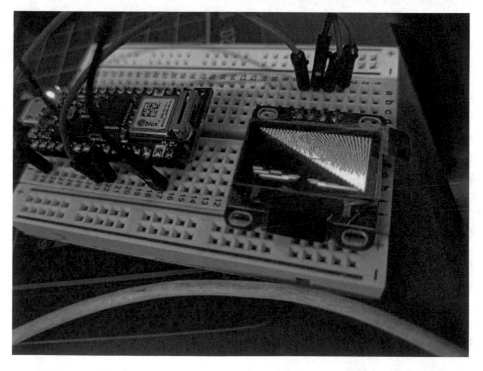

***Figure 3-13.*** *Running the ssd1306_128x64_i2c program on the OLED I2C display*

If you can see display output with the ssd1306_128x64_i2c program, it means your OLED I2C display works. We will use this OLED to display sensor data.

97

If you don't see display output, first, check the I2C address of your OLED I2C display. Then, make sure your OLED I2C displays with display size 128x64 pixels.

# Displaying the Gyroscope Sensor

In this section, we will build the Arduino program to display the Gyroscope sensor for the OLED I2C display. We will use a program from the previous section to read the Gyroscope sensor.

Now we can open Arduino software and create a new program. We start by importing all required libraries for the OLED I2C display and the Gyroscope sensor.

```
#include <SPI.h>
#include <Wire.h>
#include <Adafruit_GFX.h>
#include <Adafruit_SSD1306.h>
#include <Arduino_LSM6DS3.h>
```

We define the OLED I2C display size. In this demo, I use 128x64 pixels. You can change its size based on your OLED module.

```
#define SCREEN_WIDTH 128
#define SCREEN_HEIGHT 64
```

Next, we configure Adafruit_SSD1306 with passing the I2C address of the OLED module and display size.

```
#define OLED_RESET    4 // Reset pin
Adafruit_SSD1306 display(SCREEN_WIDTH, SCREEN_HEIGHT, &Wire,
OLED_RESET);
```

On the setup() function, we initialize serial communication, the Gyroscope sensor, and Adafruit_SSD1306.

```
void setup() {
  Serial.begin(115200);

  if (!IMU.begin()) {
    Serial.println("Failed to initialize IMU!");
    while (1);
  }
  if(!display.begin(SSD1306_SWITCHCAPVCC, 0x3C)) { // Address
0x3D for 128x64
    Serial.println(F("SSD1306 allocation failed"));
    for(;;); // Don't proceed, loop forever
  }
```

After that, we test the OLED I2C display by calling display() for 2 seconds. Then, we clear the screen of the OLED display.

```
  display.display();
  delay(2000); // Pause for 2 seconds

  // Clear the buffer
  display.clearDisplay();
}
```

On the loop() function, we read the Gyroscope sensor. First, we check the sensor data with IMU.gyroscopeAvaliable(). If it's available, we can read the sensor data using the IMU.readGyroscope() function. Store all the sensor data on the x, y, and z variables.

```
void loop() {
  float x, y, z;

  if (IMU.gyroscopeAvailable()) {
    IMU.readGyroscope(x, y, z);
```

Next, we display sensor data on the OLED I2C display using the print() function. We also use setTextSize() to set font size.

```
display.clearDisplay();
display.setTextSize(1);
display.setTextColor(SSD1306_WHITE);
display.setCursor(0,0);
display.print("Gyroscope: X, Y, Z");
display.setTextSize(2);
display.setCursor(0,12);
display.print(String(x));
display.setCursor(0,30);
display.print(String(y));
display.setCursor(0,48);
display.print(String(z));
display.display();
```

Finally, we display the sensor data into serial terminal using the Serial.print() and Serial.println() functions.

```
Serial.print(x);
Serial.print('\t');
Serial.print(y);
Serial.print('\t');
Serial.println(z);

delay(300);
  }
}
```

Save this program as OledSensor. Now you can compile and upload this program in Arduino Nano 33 IoT. You should see sensor data on the OLED I2C display, as shown in Figure 3-14.

**Figure 3-14.** *Displaying the Gyroscope sensor on the OLED I2C display*

You also can see program output on the Serial Monitor tool. You can see my program output in Figure 3-15.

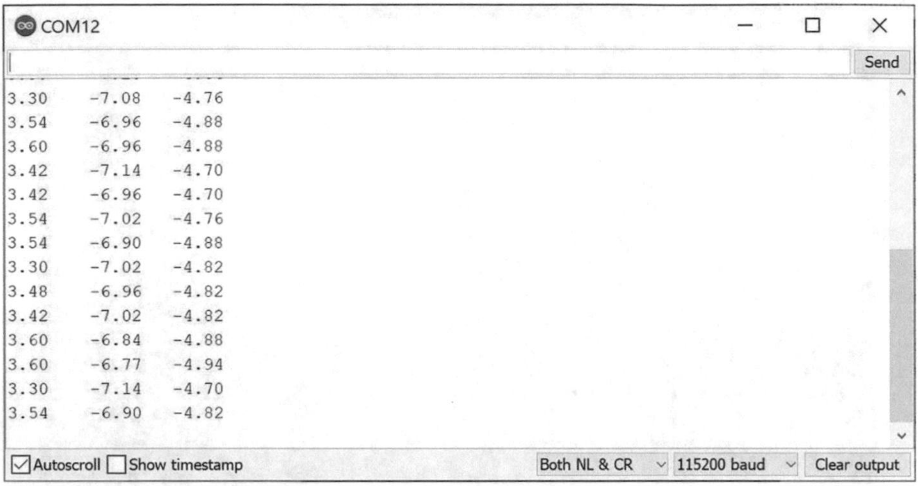

**Figure 3-15.** *Program output from OledSensor*

This is the end of the chapter. You can practice by applying the IMU sensor in your projects.

# Summary

You have learned how to access internal IMU sensors in Arduino Nano 33 IoT. We began by setting up the LSM6DS3 library. Then, we created Arduino programs to access accelerator and gyroscope sensors on Arduino Nano 33 IoT. Finally, we displayed sensor data on the Serial Plotter tool and OLED I2C display.

Next, we will learn how to access networks on Arduino Nano 33 IoT and make IoT programs.

# CHAPTER 4

# Arduino Nano 33 IoT Networking

Arduino Nano 33 IoT is designed for IoT implementation. This board has a network module, WiFi, which enables communication with other systems. In this chapter, we focus on how Arduino Nano 33 IoT accesses and collaborates with external systems, such as servers.

You will learn the following topics in this chapter:

- Setting up WiFi with WiFiNINA library

- Scanning WiFI hotspots

- Connecting to a network

- Accessing network time protocol (NTP) servers

- Building a simple IoT application

This chapter requires an environment such as a WiFi network. You should provide a WiFi hotspot with enabled Internet so Arduino Nano 33 IoT can communicate with other systems.

© Agus Kurniawan 2021
A. Kurniawan, *Beginning Arduino Nano 33 IoT*,
https://doi.org/10.1007/978-1-4842-6446-1_4

# Introduction

Arduino Nano 33 IoT is one of IoT platforms from Arduino. This board uses WiFi and Bluetooth modules to connect to a network. WiFi is a common network that people use to access the Internet. Bluetooth is a part of the wireless personal network (WPAN) that enables communication with other devices within a short distance.

***Figure 4-1.*** *WiFi module on Arduino Nano 33 IoT*

Arduino Nano 33 IoT is designed for low-cost IoT devices to leverage IoT solutions. Arduino Nano 33 IoT has a WiFi module, as shown in Figure 4-1. In this chapter, we apply a WiFi module in Arduino Nano 33 IoT to communicate with others.

# Set up the WiFiNINA Library

To access the WiFi module on the Arduino Nano 33 IoT board, we should install the WiFiNINA library. We can install it via Library Manager. You can click the menu Sketch ➤ Include Library ➤ Manage Libraries. After we click the menu for Manage Libraries, we will obtain a dialog as shown in Figure 4-2. You can type WiFiNINA in te search textbox. After that, you should see WiFiNINA on the list (see Figure 4-2).

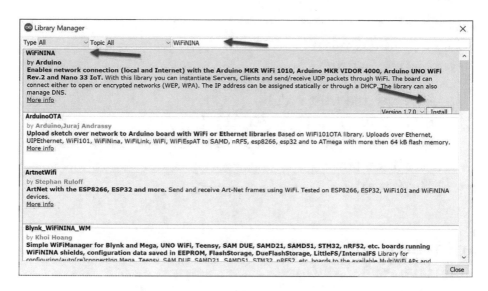

**Figure 4-2.** *Installing the WiFiNINA library*

Make sure your computer is connected to the Internet. After you install the WiFiNINA library, we can create Arduino programs to communicate with other systems over the WiFi network.

# Scanning WiFi Hotspot

We can access a WiFi hotspot if we know the WiFi SSID name. In this section, we build an Arduino program to scan existing WiFi SSIDs and then print the list on the serial terminal.

Now you can open Arduino software. You can write the following completed program.

```
#include <SPI.h>
#include <WiFiNINA.h>

int led = 13;
```

```
void setup() {
  Serial.begin(115200);
  pinMode(led, OUTPUT);

  // check for the WiFi module:
  if (WiFi.status() == WL_NO_MODULE) {
    Serial.println("Communication with WiFi module failed!");
    // don't continue
    while (true);
  }
}
void loop() {
  digitalWrite(led, HIGH);
  scanWiFi();
  digitalWrite(led, LOW);
  delay(15000);
}

void scanWiFi() {
  Serial.print("Scanning...");
  byte ssid = WiFi.scanNetworks();

  Serial.print("found ");
  Serial.println(ssid);

  for (int i = 0; i<ssid; i++) {
    Serial.print(">> ");
    Serial.print(WiFi.SSID(i));
    Serial.print("\tRSSI: ");
    Serial.print(WiFi.RSSI(i));
    Serial.print(" dBm");
    Serial.print("\tEncryption: ");
    Serial.println(WiFi.encryptionType(i));
  }
```

```
Serial.println("");
Serial.println("");
}
```

Save this program as WifiScan. Now you can compile and upload this program into Arduino Nano 33 IoT. We can see program output using the Serial Monitor.

Figure 4-3 shows my program output for the WifiScan program. You can see a list of WiFi SSIDs. If you don't see a list of WiFi SSIDs, you should move to a place where you are certain they can be found.

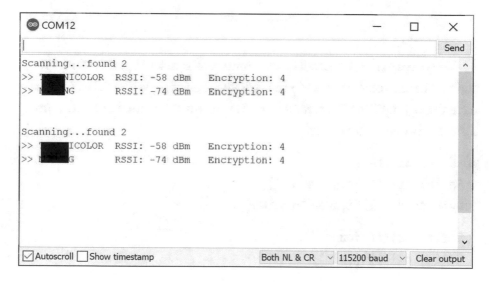

*Figure 4-3.* *Scanning WiFi hotspots*

How does it work?

First, we define the WiFiNINA library and digital pin for built-in LED on Arduino Nano 33 IoT.

```
#include <SPI.h>
#include <WiFiNINA.h>

int led = 13;
```

On setup() function, we initialize Serial and WiFi objects.

```
void setup() {
  Serial.begin(115200);
  pinMode(led, OUTPUT);

  // check for the WiFi module:
  if (WiFi.status() == WL_NO_MODULE) {
    Serial.println("Communication with WiFi module failed!");
    // don't continue
    while (true);
  }
}
```

To scan existing WiFi SSIDs, we create the scanWiFi() function. We can call WiFi.scanNetworks() to retrieve all existing WiFi SSIDs. Once we have the list of WiFi SSIDs, we print WiFi information such as SSID name, RSSI, and encryption model.

```
void scanWiFi() {
  Serial.print("Scanning...");
  byte ssid = WiFi.scanNetworks();

  Serial.print("found ");
  Serial.println(ssid);

  for (int i = 0; i<ssid; i++) {
    Serial.print(">> ");
    Serial.print(WiFi.SSID(i));
    Serial.print("\tRSSI: ");
    Serial.print(WiFi.RSSI(i));
    Serial.print(" dBm");
    Serial.print("\tEncryption: ");
    Serial.println(WiFi.encryptionType(i));
  }
```

```
Serial.println("");
Serial.println("");
}
```

We will use the scanWiFi() function in the loop() function. We can also turn on LED while the program is scanning WiFi SSIDs. After completely scanning WiFi SSIDs, we turn off the LED and set the delay for 15 seconds.

```
void loop() {
  digitalWrite(led, HIGH);
  scanWiFi();
  digitalWrite(led, LOW);
  delay(15000);
}
```

# Connecting to a WiFi Network

We already learned how to obtain a list of WiFi SSIDs. Now we can connect and join with a certain WiFI SSID. We need information about the WiFi SSID name and its key if that WiFi SSID applies an access security.

For our demo, we use the Arduino program, called WiFiWebClient. This program will connect to the WiFi SSID and then access the Google website. Figure 4-4 is a program sample: WiFiWebClient.

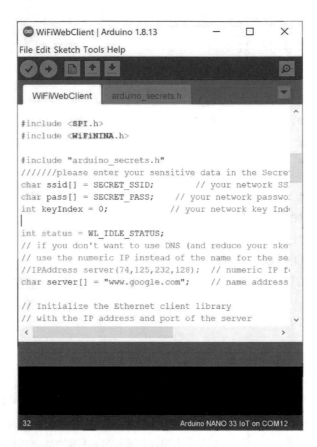

***Figure 4-4.*** *WiFiWebClient application*

You can see this project has two files: WiFiWebClient.ino and arduino_secret.h. You can set your WiFi SSID name and key on arduino_secret.h file.

```
#define SECRET_SSID "SSID"
#define SECRET_PASS "SSID-PIN"
```

Our core program is implemented in the WiFiWebClient.ino file. First, we declare WiFiNINA, WiFi SSID information, and WiFiClient objects. We also define the targeted server for the Google website like "www.google.com."

```
#include <SPI.h>
#include <WiFiNINA.h>

#include "arduino_secrets.h"
char ssid[] = SECRET_SSID;
char pass[] = SECRET_PASS;
int keyIndex = 0;

int status = WL_IDLE_STATUS;
char server[] = "www.google.com";

WiFiClient client;
```

We initialize Serial and WiFi objects. We set baudrate 115200 for serial communication. We also verify the WiFi module by calling the WiFi. status() function.

```
void setup() {
  Serial.begin(115200);
  while (!Serial) {
    ;
  }
  // check for the WiFi module:
  if (WiFi.status() == WL_NO_MODULE) {
    Serial.println("Communication with WiFi module failed!");
    // don't continue
    while (true);
  }
}
```

After the WiFi object is initialized, Arduino connects to the WiFi network. Once our Arduino is connected, we print the WiFi connection status on the serial terminal using the printWiFiStatus() function.

```
  // attempt to connect to Wifi network:
  while (status != WL_CONNECTED) {
    Serial.print("Attempting to connect to SSID: ");
    Serial.println(ssid);
    status = WiFi.begin(ssid, pass);

    // wait 10 seconds for connection:
    delay(10000);
  }
  Serial.println("Connected to wifi");
  printWifiStatus();
```

Then, we connect to Google website using the client.connect() function. After connected to Google website, we can make an HTTP GET request.

```
  Serial.println("\nStarting connection to server...");
  if (client.connect(server, 80)) {
    Serial.println("connected to server");
    // Make a HTTP request:
    client.println("GET /search?q=arduino HTTP/1.1");
    client.println("Host: www.google.com");
    client.println("Connection: close");
    client.println();
  }
}

void loop() {
  while (client.available()) {
    char c = client.read();
    Serial.write(c);
  }
```

```
// if the server's disconnected, stop the client:
if (!client.connected()) {
  Serial.println();
  Serial.println("disconnecting from server.");
  client.stop();

  // do nothing forevermore:
  while (true);
  }
}
```

The following is an implementation of the printWiFiStatus()
function. We print the IP address using the WiFi.localIP() function. We
also obtain RSSI by calling the WiFi.RSSI() function.

```
void printWifiStatus() {
  // print the SSID of the network you're attached to:
  Serial.print("SSID: ");
  Serial.println(WiFi.SSID());

  // print your WiFi shield's IP address:
  IPAddress ip = WiFi.localIP();
  Serial.print("IP Address: ");
  Serial.println(ip);

  // print the received signal strength:
  long rssi = WiFi.RSSI();
  Serial.print("signal strength (RSSI):");
  Serial.print(rssi);
  Serial.println(" dBm");
}
```

Save all codes. Now you can compile and upload this program into
Arduino Nano 33 IoT. We can see program output using Serial Monitor.

Figure 4-5 shows my program output for the WiFiWebClient program. You can see the output program by accessing the Google website.

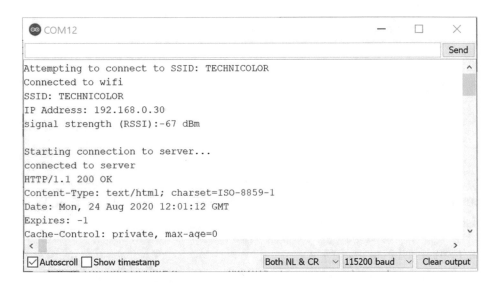

**Figure 4-5.** *Programming output for accessing the Google website*

# Accessing Network Time Protocol Server

Sometimes we want to get current time on Arduino Nano 33 IoT. We can apply the network time protocol (NTP) server to retrieve current time. This time uses the UTC timezone.

For our demo, we can use a program sample from Arduino. This program is called WiFiUdpNtpClient. You can see this program in Figure 4-6.

We will explore this program. First, this program has two files: WiFiUdpNtpClient.ino and arduino_secret.h. You can set your WiFi SSID name and key on arduino_secret.h file.

```
#define SECRET_SSID "SSID"
#define SECRET_PASS "SSID-PIN"
```

Our core program is implemented in the WiFiUdpNtpClient.ino file. We declare WiFiNINA, WiFi SSID information, and WiFiClient objects.

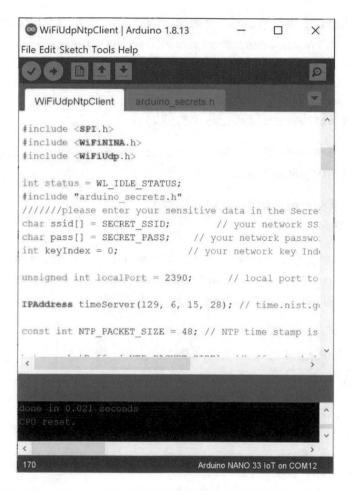

***Figure 4-6.*** *Program codes for WiFiUdpNtpClient*

```
#include <SPI.h>
#include <WiFiNINA.h>
#include <WiFiUdp.h>

int status = WL_IDLE_STATUS;
#include "arduino_secrets.h"
char ssid[] = SECRET_SSID;
char pass[] = SECRET_PASS;
int keyIndex = 0;
```

We must also define the NTP server. We connect to 192.6.15.28 for time.nist.gov. We initialize packet size and WiFiUDP object.

```
unsigned int localPort = 2390;
// time.nist.gov NTP server
IPAddress timeServer(129, 6, 15, 28);

// NTP time stamp is in the first 48 bytes of the message
const int NTP_PACKET_SIZE = 48;

byte packetBuffer[ NTP_PACKET_SIZE];
WiFiUDP Udp;
```

On the setup() function, we initialize serial communication and WiFi object. Once we have connected to the WiFi network, we can initialize the UDP protocol by calling Udp.begin().

```
void setup() {
  Serial.begin(9600);
  while (!Serial) {
    ; // wait for serial port to connect. Needed for native USB
        port only
  }

  // check for the WiFi module:
  if (WiFi.status() == WL_NO_MODULE) {
    Serial.println("Communication with WiFi module failed!");
    // don't continue
    while (true);
  }

  String fv = WiFi.firmwareVersion();
  if (fv < "1.0.0") {
    Serial.println("Please upgrade the firmware");
  }
```

```
// attempt to connect to Wifi network:
while (status != WL_CONNECTED) {
  Serial.print("Attempting to connect to SSID: ");
  Serial.println(ssid);
  // Connect to WPA/WPA2 network. Change this line if using
      open or WEP network:
  status = WiFi.begin(ssid, pass);

  // wait 10 seconds for connection:
  delay(10000);
}

Serial.println("Connected to wifi");
printWifiStatus();

Serial.println("\nStarting connection to server...");
Udp.begin(localPort);
}
```

On the loop() function, we send data to the NTP server by calling the sendNTPpacket() function. We will implement the sendNTPpacket() function in the next step. Once we have a response from the NTP server, we parse data using Udp.parsePacket().

```
void loop() {
  sendNTPpacket(timeServer);
  delay(1000);
  if (Udp.parsePacket()) {
    Serial.println("packet received");
    Udp.read(packetBuffer, NTP_PACKET_SIZE);
```

We calculate epoch time from the NTP server to be second numbers.

```
unsigned long highWord = word(packetBuffer[40],
packetBuffer[41]);
unsigned long lowWord = word(packetBuffer[42],
packetBuffer[43]);

unsigned long secsSince1900 = highWord << 16 | lowWord;
Serial.print("Seconds since Jan 1 1900 = ");
Serial.println(secsSince1900);

// now convert NTP time into everyday time:
Serial.print("Unix time = ");
// Unix time starts on Jan 1 1970. In seconds, that's
    2208988800:
const unsigned long seventyYears = 2208988800UL;
// subtract seventy years:
unsigned long epoch = secsSince1900 - seventyYears;
// print Unix time:
Serial.println(epoch);
```

Then, we print UTC time, such as hour, minute, and second to the serial terminal.

```
Serial.print("The UTC time is ");
Serial.print((epoch  % 86400L) / 3600);
Serial.print(':');
if (((epoch % 3600) / 60) < 10) {
  Serial.print('0');
}
Serial.print((epoch  % 3600) / 60);
Serial.print(':');
if ((epoch % 60) < 10) {
  Serial.print('0');
}
```

```
    Serial.println(epoch % 60); // print the second
  }
  delay(10000);
}
```

The following is an implementation of the sendNTPpacket() function. We request data from the NTP server. We pass the IP address of the NTP server. A result of the NTP response is read and stored to the packetBuffer variable.

```
unsigned long sendNTPpacket(IPAddress& address) {
  // set all bytes in the buffer to 0
  memset(packetBuffer, 0, NTP_PACKET_SIZE);
  // Initialize values needed to form NTP request
  packetBuffer[0] = 0b11100011;   // LI, Version, Mode
  packetBuffer[1] = 0;      // Stratum, or type of clock
  packetBuffer[2] = 6;      // Polling Interval
  packetBuffer[3] = 0xEC;   // Peer Clock Precision
  // 8 bytes of zero for Root Delay & Root Dispersion
  packetBuffer[12]  = 49;
  packetBuffer[13]  = 0x4E;
  packetBuffer[14]  = 49;
  packetBuffer[15]  = 52;

  //NTP requests are to port 123
  Udp.beginPacket(address, 123);
  Udp.write(packetBuffer, NTP_PACKET_SIZE);
  Udp.endPacket();
}
```

The following is an implementation of the printWiFiStatus() function. We print the IP address using the WiFi.localIP() function. We also obtain RSSI by calling the WiFi.RSSI() function.

```
void printWifiStatus() {
  // print the SSID of the network you're attached to:
  Serial.print("SSID: ");
  Serial.println(WiFi.SSID());

  // print your WiFi shield's IP address:
  IPAddress ip = WiFi.localIP();
  Serial.print("IP Address: ");
  Serial.println(ip);

  // print the received signal strength:
  long rssi = WiFi.RSSI();
  Serial.print("signal strength (RSSI):");
  Serial.print(rssi);
  Serial.println(" dBm");
}
```

Now we can save this program. You can compile and upload to Arduino Nano 33 IoT. Then, open the Serial Monitor tool to see the program output. Figure 4-7 shows my program output.

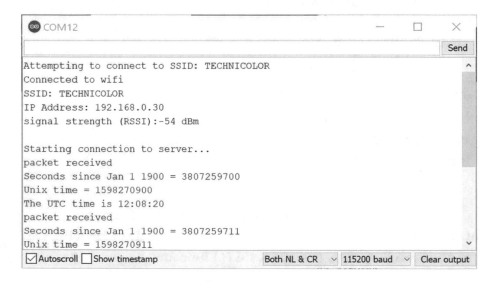

***Figure 4-7.*** *Program output for getting current time from the NTP server*

# Building a Simple IoT Application

Since we have a network module in Arduino Nano 33 IoT, we can build a simple IoT application. We can control an LED from a website. We can turn on/off LEDs. For demo implementation, we need three LEDs.

Technically, we will build a simple webserver inside Arduino Nano 33 IoT. We receive HTTP GET requests to perform LED on/off from users. We define the following HTTP GET requests.

- http://<ip_address Arduino>/gpio1/1 for turning on LED1

- http://<ip_address Arduino>/gpio1/0 for turning off LED1

- http://<ip_address Arduino>/gpio2/1 for turning on LED2

- http://<ip_address Arduino>/gpio2/0 for turning on LED2

- http://<ip_address Arduino>/gpio3/1 for turning on LED3

- http://<ip_address Arduino>/gpio3/0 for turning on LED3

Next, we build wiring for our demo.

## Wiring

We need three LEDs for our demo. We can build the following wiring:

- LED 1 is connected to digital pin 6 on Arduino Nano 33 IoT

- LED 2 is connected to digital pin 4 on Arduino Nano 33 IoT.

- LED 3 is connected to digital pin 3 on Arduino Nano 33 IoT.

- All LED GND pins are connected to ground (GND) pin on Arduino Nano 33 IoT.

Figure 4-8 shows our wiring for the IoT project.

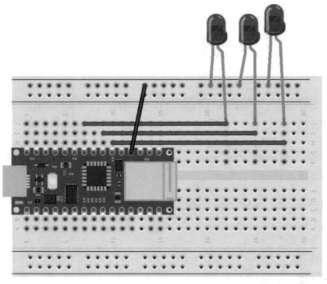

**Figure 4-8.** *Wiring for the IoT project*

# Developing Program

Our IoT project implementation is to build the Arduino program with Sketch. We will connect to existing WiFi and then perform a simple web server. We must wait for incoming HTTP GET requests to turn on/off LEDs.

To implement, we open Arduino software and create a new project. First, we define our LED pins and WiFi SSIDs. Set your WiFi SSID name and SSID key if it's available. To implement a simple web server, we use the WiFiServer library. You can read it at this link, https://www.arduino.cc/en/Reference/WiFiServer.

```
#include <SPI.h>
#include <WiFiNINA.h>

int led1 = 6;
int led2 = 4;
int led3 = 3;

const char* ssid = "wifi-ssid";
const char* password = "ssid-key";

int status = WL_IDLE_STATUS;
WiFiServer server(80);
```

On the setup() function, we initialize Serial object with baudrate 115200 and set digital mode for LED pins. We set OUTPUT for digital mode.

```
void setup() {
  Serial.begin(115200);
  delay(10);

  // prepare GPIO5
  pinMode(led1, OUTPUT);
  pinMode(led2, OUTPUT);
  pinMode(led3, OUTPUT);
  digitalWrite(led1, 0);
  digitalWrite(led2, 0);
  digitalWrite(led3, 0);
```

Next, we connect to existing WiFi by calling the WiFi.begin() function and pass WiFi SSID and its key.

```
while (status != WL_CONNECTED) {
    Serial.print("Attempting to connect to SSID: ");
    Serial.println(ssid);
    status = WiFi.begin(ssid, password);
```

```
  // wait 10 seconds for connection:
  delay(10000);
}
Serial.println("");
Serial.println("WiFi connected");
```

If our Arduino is connected to the WiFi network, we can start a web server by calling the begin() function from the WiFiServer object.

```
server.begin();
Serial.println("Server started");

// Print the IP address
char ips[24];
IPAddress ip = WiFi.localIP();
sprintf(ips, "%d.%d.%d.%d", ip[0], ip[1], ip[2], ip[3]);
Serial.println(ips);
}
```

On the loop() function, we perform some tasks such as waiting for incoming HTTP requests. Then, we parse incoming packets. If the packet is valid, we can turn on/off LED. First, we wait for incoming client connections. We can call server.available().

```
void loop() {
  // Check if a client has connected
  WiFiClient client = server.available();
  if (!client) {
    return;
  }

  // Wait until the client sends some data
  Serial.println("new client");
  while(!client.available()){
    delay(1);
  }
```

Once we have a connected client, we wait for incoming HTTP request packets. We parse the packet to identify the type of command. We can use a string manipulation process. We call indexOf() if we have "/gpioX/Y" requests. X is an LED number, and Y is a command for turning on/off LED.

```
String req = client.readStringUntil('\r');
Serial.println(req);
client.flush();

// Match the request
int val1 = 0;
int val2 = 0;
int val3 = 0;
int ledreq = 0;
if (req.indexOf("/gpio1/0") != -1) {
  val1 = 0;
  ledreq = 1;
}
else if (req.indexOf("/gpio1/1") != -1) {
  val1 = 1;
  ledreq = 1;
}
else if (req.indexOf("/gpio2/0") != -1) {
  val2 = 0;
  ledreq = 2;
}
else if (req.indexOf("/gpio2/1") != -1) {
  val2 = 1;
  req = 2;
}
else if (req.indexOf("/gpio3/0") != -1) {
  val3 = 0;
  ledreq = 3;
}
```

```
else if (req.indexOf("/gpio3/1") != -1) {
  val3 = 1;
  ledreq = 3;
}
else {
  Serial.println("invalid request");
  client.stop();
  return;
}
```

After we identify a command type, we can turn on/off LEDs using digitalWrite().

```
digitalWrite(led1, val1);
digitalWrite(led2, val2);
digitalWrite(led3, val3);
```

Next, we send a response to the client. We send HTML scripts using the client.print() function. After that, we close the client connection.

```
client.flush();
String s = "HTTP/1.1 200 OK\r\nContent-Type: text/html\r\n\r\
n<!DOCTYPE HTML>\r\n<html>\r\n";
if(ledreq==1) {
  s += "LED1 is ";
  s += (val1)? "ON": "OFF";
}else if(ledreq==2) {
  s += "LED2 is ";
  s += (val2)? "ON": "OFF";
}else if(ledreq==3) {
  s += "LED3 is ";
  s += (val3)? "ON": "OFF";
}
s += "</html>\n";
```

```
// Send the response to the client
client.print(s);
delay(1);
client.stop();
Serial.println("Client disonnected");
}
```

You can save this program as IoTDemo. Next, we can compile and test this program.

## Testing

After we compile and upload the IoTDemo program into Arduino Nano 33 IoT, we can open the Serial Monitor tool. We should see our IP address from Arduino Nano 33 IoT. If we don't have it, our Arduino Nano 33 IoT probably obtained problems while connecting to existing WiFi. Figure 4-9 shows my IP address from Arduino Nano 33 IoT.

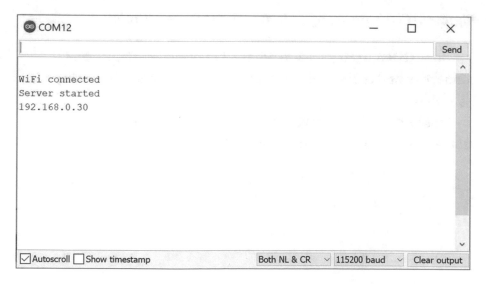

*Figure 4-9.* *Arduino Nano 33 IoT is connected to WiFi*

For testing, we can use a browser. You can make a request to turn on an LED. We can call http://<ipaddress>/gpio1/1 to turn on LED 1. If we succeed, we will obtain a response, as shown in Figure 4-10. LED 1 also is lighting.

LED1 is ON

***Figure 4-10.*** *Turning on LED over the HTTP GET request*

To turn off LED 1, we can make a request with this link, http://<ipaddress>/gpio1/0. We will see LED 1 turns off. We also obtain a response from Arduino Nano 33 IoT, as shown in Figure 4-11.

LED1 is OFF

***Figure 4-11.*** *Turning off LED over the HTTP GET request*

Our IoTDemo program also prints all information about client connection and client requests. You can see my program output in Figure 4-12.

This is the end of the chapter. We can practice by developing IoT programs based on the Arduino Nano 33 IoT board.

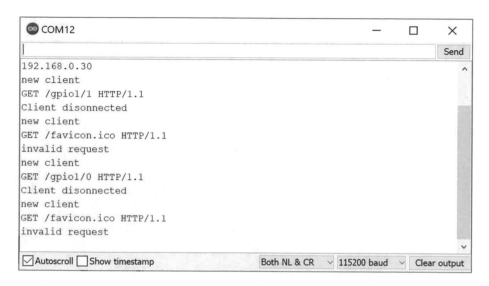

*Figure 4-12.* *Program output from the IoT project on a serial terminal*

# Summary

We already learned how to set up the WiFiNINA library on Arduino Nano 33 IoT. We connected our board to an existing WiFi network. Then, we attempted to connect to the Google website. We requested a current time from the NTP server. Finally, we built an IoT application to turn on/off LED.

In the next chapter, we will learn how to connect to Arduino IoT Cloud.

# CHAPTER 5

# Arduino IoT Cloud

Arduino IoT Cloud is one of Arduino services to provide a cloud service for an IoT platform. We can send and receive data from IoT devices to Arduino IoT Cloud. This chapter explores how Arduino Nano 33 IoT interacts with Arduino IoT Cloud.

You will learn the following topics in this chapter:

- Setting up Arduino IoT Cloud

- Building programs on Arduino Nano 33 IoT for the Arduino IoT Cloud

- Building sensor monitoring program with the Arduino IoT Cloud

## Introduction

A cloud technology enables us to enhance our IT and business productivity. A cloud technology also can be used to address IoT solutions. Arduino IoT Cloud is one of cloud servers from Arduino. We can send and receive data from Arduino IoT Cloud to our Arduino devices.

In this chapter, we build programs on Arduino Nano 33 IoT to access the Arduino IoT Cloud. Arduino Nano 33 IoT has a WiFi module so we can connect to the Arduino IoT cloud over the WiFi network. Make sure you have Internet access on WiFi network.

© Agus Kurniawan 2021
A. Kurniawan, *Beginning Arduino Nano 33 IoT*,
https://doi.org/10.1007/978-1-4842-6446-1_5

# Setting up Arduino IoT Cloud

To access and build programs for the Arduino IoT Cloud, we need to set up our Arduino devices. We should register a new account to this platform. You can register your account on Arduino IoT Cloud to this link, `https://create.arduino.cc/iot/`. After we sign up, we register our Arduino Nano 33 IoT to the Arduino IoT Cloud.

You can see the Arduino IoT Cloud dashboard in Figure 5-1. We have three menus: Things, Dashboards and Devices. Members without a paid subscription can only create the Things menu on this platform.

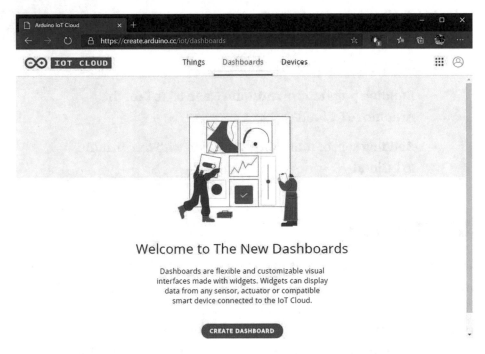

*Figure 5-1.*  *A dashboard of the Arduino IoT Cloud website*

If you have an account in the Arduino store, you can use the same account to sign up for Arduino IoT Cloud. Then, we can register our Arduino Nano 33 IoT.

# Register Arduino Nano 33 IoT

Before we use Arduino IoT Cloud, we have to register our Arduino devices. In this chapter, we use Arduino Nano 33 IoT. We have some steps to register our Arduino devices. You can perform the following tasks:

- installing Arduino Create Agent

- adding a new Arduino device

Next, we can install the Arduino Create Agent.

## Install the Arduino Create Agent

Arduino Create Agent is a background program to listen to our local Arduino devices. This agent program acts as a bridge between local Arduino devices and Arduino IoT Cloud.

The Arduino Create Agent program is available for Windows, Linux, and the macOS platform. You can download this program at this link, `https://github.com/arduino/arduino-create-agent`. After installed, you should allow this program to run in the background. On the Windows platform, you can see a tray icon for the Arduino Create Agent on the taskbar, as shown in Figure 5-2.

***Figure 5-2.*** *A tray icon of the Arduino Create Agent on Windows OS*

You can open the Debug Console menu by clicking this in the Arduino Create Agent. If your Arduino devices are attached on local computer, a debug console from the Arduino Create Agent will show our device status. Figure 5-3 shows my Arduino Nano 33 IoT is detected.

*Figure 5-3.  A form of the Arduino Create Agent Debug Console*

If you don't see your Arduino device, make sure your Arduino is attached to your computer properly. After completed, you can register your Arduino Nano 33 IoT.

## Add New Arduino Device

Once we have set up the Arduino Create Agent program on a local computer, we can add a new Arduino device. You can open the Arduino IoT Cloud website. Then, click the DEVICES menu. You can see a list of Arduino devices.

Now you can add a new Arduino Nano 33 IoT. You can plug in your Arduino Nano 33 IoT. You should see a dialog, as shown in Figure 5-4. Click Set up in the Arduino device menu.

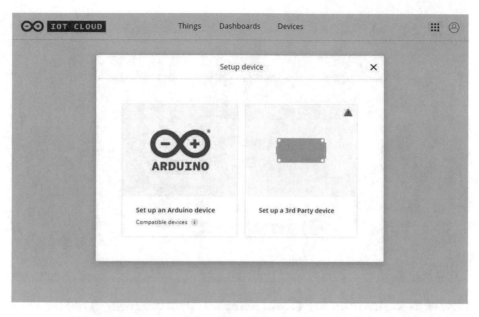

***Figure 5-4.*** *Adding a new Arduino device*

After clicking this option, you should see Arduino Nano 33 IoT, as shown in Figure 5-5. If you don't see your Arduino Nano 33 IoT, make sure your Arduino Nano 33 IoT is attached and Arduino Create Agent is running.

***Figure 5-5.*** *Arduino IoT Cloud detected Arduino Nano 33 IoT*

Set your device name for Arduino Nano 33 IoT. If done, you can click the CONFIGURE button. Arduino IoT Cloud will configure your Arduino Nano 33 IoT, as shown in Figure 5-6. It will take several minutes to complete this task. After completing configuration, you should see your Arduino Nano 33 IoT listed on the Arduino IoT Cloud list, as shown in Figure 5-7.

***Figure 5-6.*** *Configuring Arduino Nano 33 IoT*

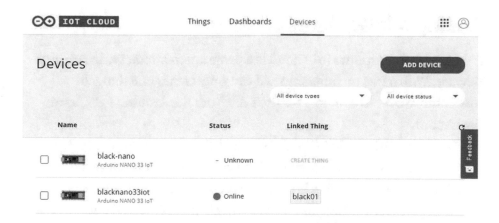

***Figure 5-7.*** *Arduino Nano 33 IoT device was added*

# Develop a Remote LED Button

In this section, we build a program to remote LED from the Arduino IoT Cloud dashboard. We can turn on/off the LED on Arduino Nano 33 IoT from the Arduino IoT Cloud dashboard website.

To implement our demo, we can perform some tasks with the following steps:

- adding a new thing
- adding properties
- editing Sketch program
- building a dashboard
- testing

We implement these steps in the next section.

## Adding a New Thing

A feature of the Arduino IoT Cloud is a program to interact with Arduino devices. With a free membership, we can only create one thing. In this demo, we build a remote for the LED from the Arduino IoT Cloud dashboard.

Open the Arduino IoT Cloud website. Click the Things menu. Then, you can obtain a form, as shown in Figure 5-8. Enter your Thing name and Arduino device. Each Thing is connected by one Arduino device.

After you set the Thing name, you can click the CREATE button. After that, you will see a form, as shown in Figure 5-9. We will configure Properties for Arduino Nano 33 IoT in the next section.

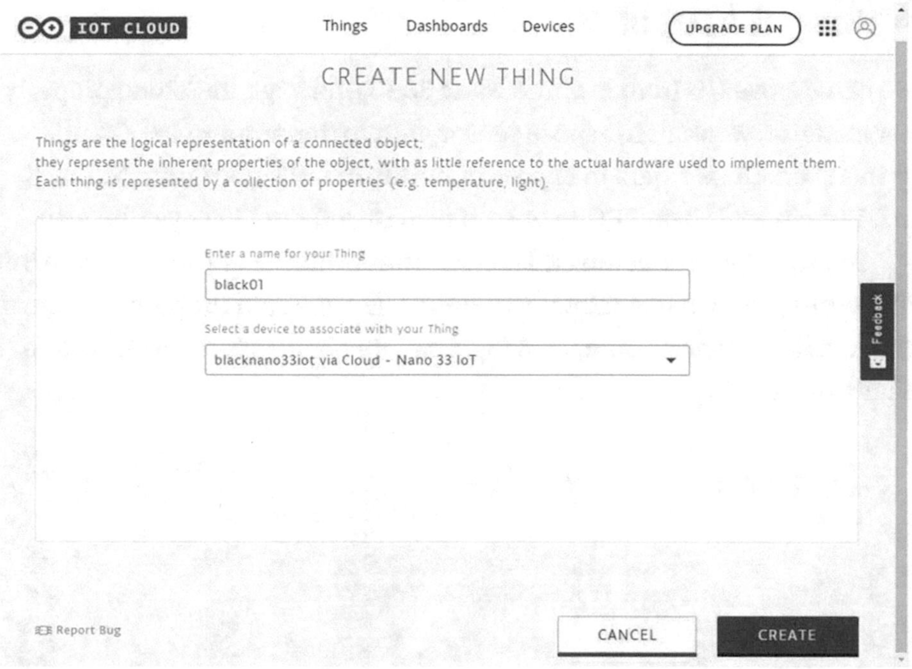

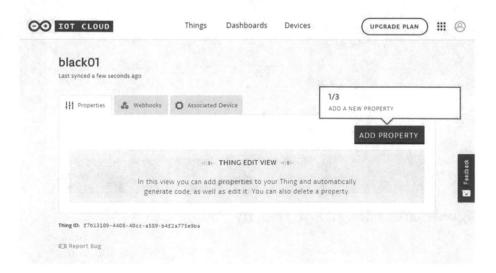

*Figure 5-8.* *Adding a new Thing*

*Figure 5-9.* *A dashboard of an Arduino Thing*

# Adding a Property

We can expose I/O from Arduino Nano 33 IoT through the Thing property. For instance, we want to expose sensor data to the Arduino IoT Cloud. In this scenario, we want to expose our built-in LED in Arduino Nano 33 IoT. We can set I/O on LED so we can turn on/off the LED over the web.

You can start by opening a Thing on the Arduino IoT Cloud. Figure 5-9 shows our Thing that we already created. Click the Add Property button to add a new property. After clicking, you will obtain a form, as shown in Figure 5-10.

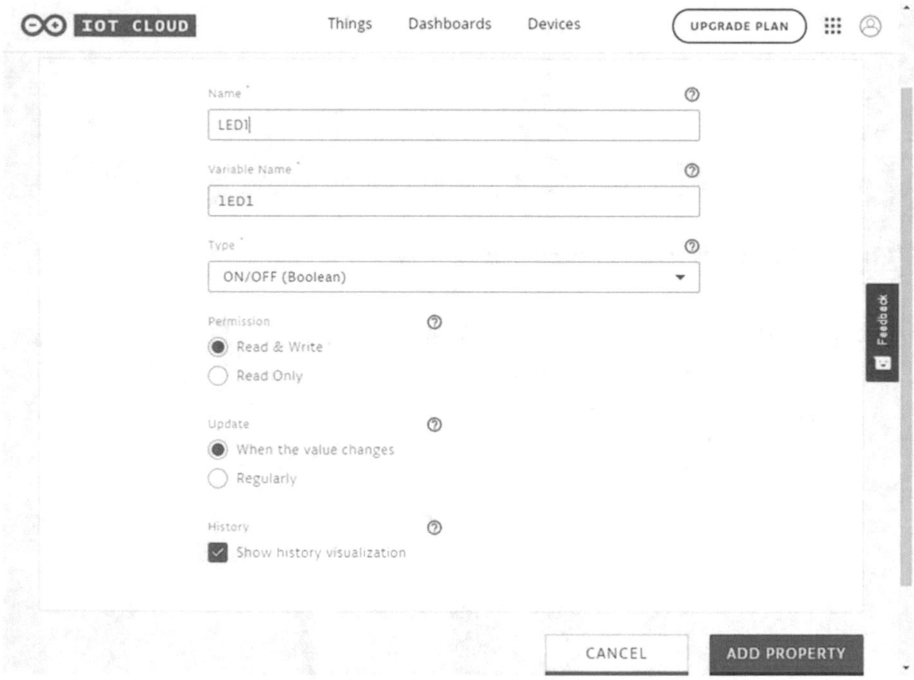

*Figure 5-10.* *Adding a new property*

In this scenario, you can set the following options:

- Name: LED1

- VARIABLE NAME: lED1

- TYPE: ON/OFF (Boolean)

- Permission: Read & Write

- Update: when the value changes

- History: checked

My entry is shown in Figure 5-10. After filled all fields, you can click the ADD PROPERTY button. You will come back to the Things form. You should see LED1 property on the Thing form, as shown in Figure 5-11.

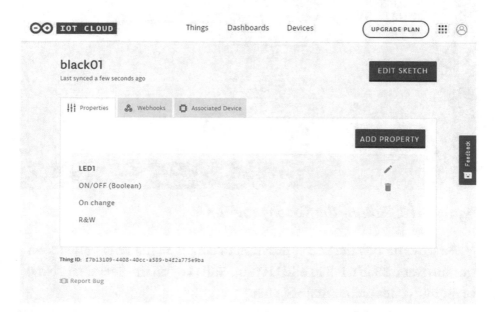

*Figure 5-11.*  *A Thing with one property*

You have created a Thing. Next, we can modify the Sketch program in order to connect to this LED1 property.

# Editing the Sketch Program

Now we can edit our Sketch program. On the property form from the Thing dashboard (see Figure 5-11), you can click the EDIT SKETCH button. After clicking, you will obtain the Arduino web editor, as shown in Figure 5-12.

***Figure 5-12.*** *Editing the Sketch program*

First, we modify the Secret program to configure the WiFi network on Arduino Nano 33 IoT. Fill in SSID ID and SSID key on the Secret tab. Now we modify codes on our main Sketch.

You can see our property variable, lED1, is declared on the main Sketch program.

```
#include "arduino_secrets.h"
  bool lED1;
#include "thingProperties.h"
```

Then, we initialize our digital pin for a built-in LED. We also set
lED1=false for initialization. We add the following script on the setup()
function.

```
void setup() {
...

  lED1 = false;
  pinMode(13,OUTPUT);

....
}
```

On the onLED1Change() function, we perform turn on/off LED. If
we have lED1=true, we turn on the LED by calling the digitalWrite()
function. Otherwise, we turn off the LED.

```
void onLED1Change() {
  // Do something
  if(lED1)
     digitalWrite(13, HIGH);
  else
     digitalWrite(13, LOW);
}
```

Save this program. You can compile and upload this program to
Arduino Nano 33 IoT. Click Verify and Upload icons for compiling and
uploading program.

# Build a Dashboard

Now we can build a dashboard that is used to create interaction between
Arduino IoT Cloud and Arduino Nano 33 IoT. We can create many
dashboards for a Thing project. In our scenario, we create a dashboard
with a button. First, click the DASHBOARD menu. Create a new dashboard
so you will obtain a form, as shown in Figure 5-13.

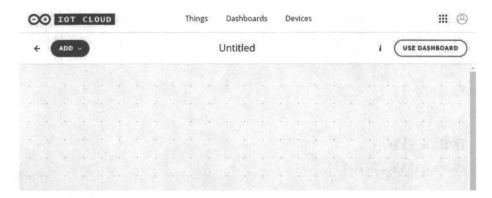

Figure 5-13. *A dashboard of Arduino IoT Cloud*

We can add a new switch on our dashboard editor. Click the ADD button and select Switch widget. You can see the Switch widget option in Figure 5-14.

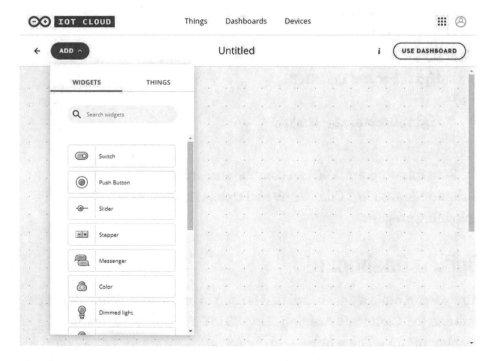

Figure 5-14. *Adding a widget on the dashboard*

144

Click Switch widget and then drag it to the dashboard editor. After dragging the Switch widget, you should see Switch widget, as shown in Figure 5-15.

Click Example Data to link the Switch widget to the Thing property. After clicking, you will obtain a form as shown in Figure 5-16.

**Figure 5-15.** *Adding a switch*

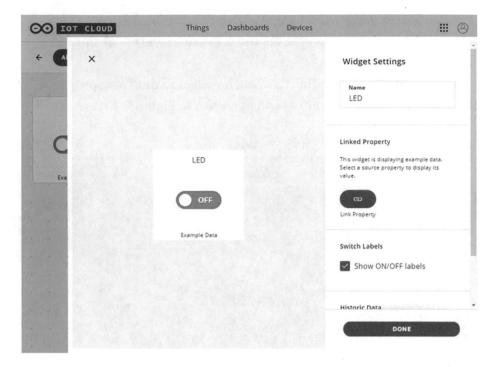

***Figure 5-16.*** *Setting a Switch widget*

Click the Linked Property button to link with the Thing property. We will obtain a form, as shown in Figure 5-17. Select our Thing name, and select Property (LED1). If done, click the LINK PROPERTY button. Then, we will back to our dashboard editor.

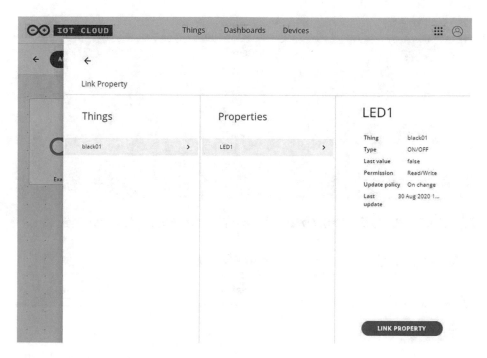

*Figure 5-17.* *Linking a switch to thing properties*

You also can rename our dashboard program—for instance, LED Demo. Now we can test our dashboard program.

# Testing

To test our program, we need to activate our dashboard program on running mode. You can click the USE DASHBORD button to activate the dashboard program.

You can attempt to toggle the Switch to ON mode. Then, you should see the built-in LED on Arduino Nano 33 IoT lights up. You also can turn off the LED by toggling the Switch to OFF mode.

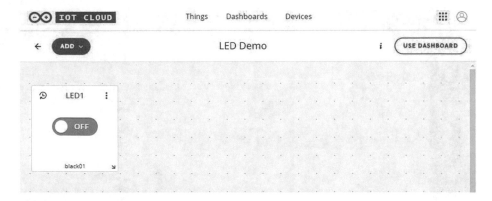

*Figure 5-18.* *LED demo program on the dashboard editor*

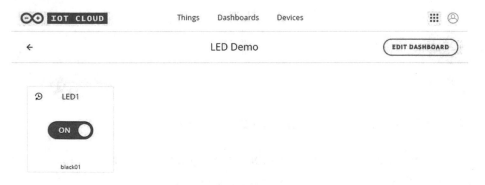

*Figure 5-19.* *Toggling the Switch to turn on the LED*

You can customize this program by adding some LEDs. Then, you can add some properties on the Things program.

# Develop Sensor Monitoring

We have created Arduino IoT Cloud to turn on/off LED on Arduino Nano 33 IoT. Now we can continue to build the Arduino IoT Cloud program for monitoring sensors. In this demo, we use built-in sensors on Arduino Nano 33 IoT. For testing, we use the Gyroscope sensor.

To implement this demo, we can perform some tasks with the following steps:

- adding a new thing
- adding properties
- editing the Sketch program
- building a dashboard
- testing

We implement these steps in the next section.

## Add a New Thing

You can create a new Thing on Arduino IoT Cloud. If you have a free membership, you should delete the existing Thing on Arduino IoT Cloud because you can only create one Thing.

Now you can create a new Thing. For instance, we set the Thing name as GyroscropeThing. Then, we can add some properties to GyroscopeThing.

## Add Property

After creating a Thing, we can add properties. For this demo, we create three properties to monitor the Gyroscope sensor from Arduino Nano 33 IoT. These properties will be linked to X, Y, and Z degrees from the Gyroscope sensor. When we can add a new property, we have a form, as shown in Figure 5-20. We add three properties with property parameters as shown in Table 5-1.

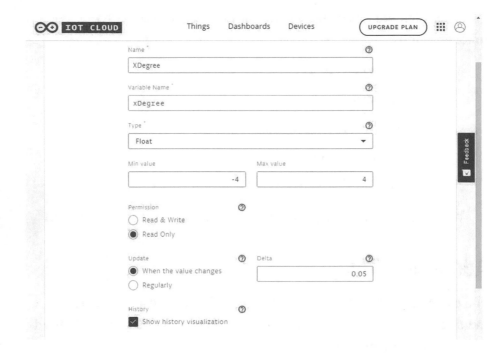

***Figure 5-20.** Adding a property on a Thing*

***Table 5-1.** Input Paramters for Three Thing Properties*

| Parameters | Property 1 | Property 2 | Property 3 |
| --- | --- | --- | --- |
| Name | xDegree | yDegree | zDegree |
| Variable | xDegree | yDegree | zDegree |
| Type | Float | Float | Float |
| Minimum/Maximum | -4/-4 | -4/-4 | -4/-4 |
| Permission | Read-only | Read-only | Read-only |
| Update | | | |
| Delta | 0.05 | 0.05 | 0.05 |
| Show history visualization | Checked | Checked | Checked |

After we creat three Thing properties, we will return to our Things dashboard. You can see three properties in Figure 5-21.

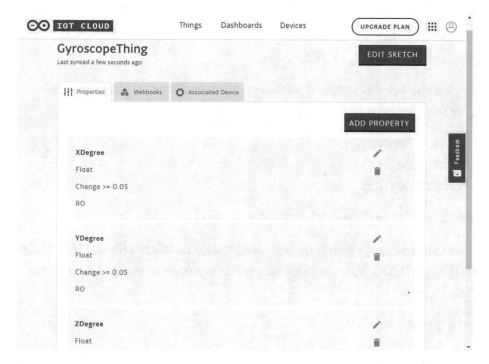

**Figure 5-21.** *Three properties on GyroscopeThing*

# Editing the Sketch Program

After we add three properties on GyroscopeThing, we can edit the Sketch program. We will read the gyroscope sensor and then update sensor data to property variables.

Click the EDIT SKETCH button to edit our program on Arduino IoT Cloud. Then, we have the Sketch web editor. We modify this Sketch program to enable us to read the Gyroscope sensor and update three Thing properties.

First, we set the SSID ID and SSID key on Arduino Secret. Then, we open the main program. We add the LSM6DS3 library on the Sketch program.

```
#include "arduino_secrets.h"
#include <Arduino_LSM6DS3.h>
```

We will see our property variables, such as xDegree, yDegree, and zDegree.

```
  float xDegree;
  float yDegree;
  float zDegree;
```

```
#include "thingProperties.h"
```

On the setup() function, we initialize the LSM6DS3 library by calling IMU.begin() API. Then, we can access the Gyroscope sensor on Arduino Nano 33 IoT.

```
void setup() {
...
  if (!IMU.begin()) {
    Serial.println("Failed to initialize IMU!");

    while (1);
  }
...
}
```

We can read the Gyroscope sensor and then update to xDegree, yDegree, and zDegree variables. We can call IMU.gyroscopeAvailable() to check whether sensor data is available or not. To read sensor data, we can use the IMU.readGyroscope() function.

```
void loop() {
  ArduinoCloud.update();
  // Your code here
  if (IMU.gyroscopeAvailable()) {
    IMU.readGyroscope(xDegree, yDegree, zDegree);
  }
  delay(1000);
}
```

Save this program. Now you can compile this Sketch program and upload to Arduino Nano 33 IoT device.

## Build a Dashboard

We build a dashboard to create interaction between Arduino Nano 33 IoT and Arduino IoT Cloud. We perform a new dashboard program with the following steps:

- Create a new dashboard.

- Add three value widgets into the dashboard editor.

- Each value widget is to be linked to each Thing Property, as shown in Figure 5-22.

- Do the same action for XDegree, YDegree, and ZDegree value widgets.

Last, we can set dashboard name. Now we can test our widgets on the dashboard.

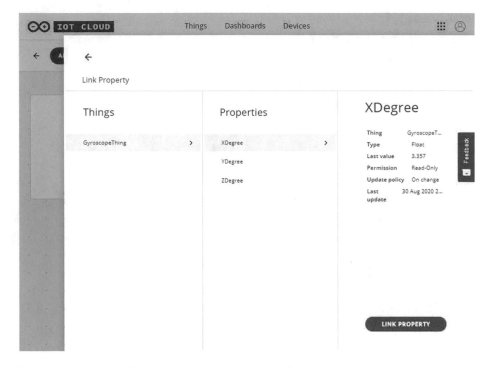

***Figure 5-22.*** *Linking a property to a widget*

# Testing

We can test our Arduino IoT Cloud program. You can navigate to the Arduino IoT Cloud dashboard. Click the dashboard form that we already created. Click the USE DASHBORD button to be in RUN mode.

You can see the widget output in Figure 5-23. Shake your Arduino Nano 33 IoT board to see sensor data changes on dashboard widgets.

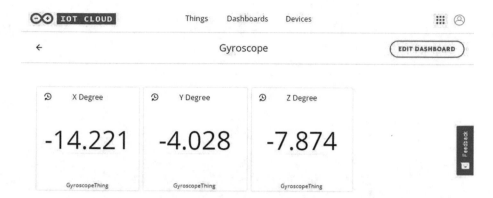

***Figure 5-23.*** *Showing sensor values on the Arduino IoT Cloud dashboard*

You have created a dashboard on Arduino IoT Cloud to monitor sensors from Arduino Nano 33 IoT. You can practice by applying some sensors or actuators to integrate with Arduino IoT Cloud.

# Summary

We have learned how to get started with Arduino IoT Cloud. We have set up and registered our Arduino Nano 33 IoT to Arduino IoT Cloud. We also have built two programs for Arduino IoT Cloud: remoting an LED and sensor monitoring.

Next, we will learn how to work and make interaction with Bluetooth Low Energy.

# CHAPTER 6

# Bluetooth Low Energy (BLE)

Arduino Nano 33 IoT has two built-in network modules: WiFi and Bluetooth. In this chapter, we explore how to get started with Bluetooth Low Energy (BLE) on Arduino Nano 33 IoT. We will build programs to utilize the BLE module.

You will learn the following topics in this chapter:

- Setting up BLE library on Arduino Nano 33 IoT

- Building a simple BLE application

- Developing an LED control program over BLE

- Exposing sensor data over BLE service

## Introduction

Arduino Nano 33 IoT is one of the IoT platforms from Arduino. This board uses WiFi and Bluetooth modules to connect to a network. Arduino Nano 33 IoT has support for BLE radio. BLE technology enables us to advertise our services and make interactions among BLE devices such as mobile devices.

© Agus Kurniawan 2021
A. Kurniawan, *Beginning Arduino Nano 33 IoT*,
https://doi.org/10.1007/978-1-4842-6446-1_6

Each BLE radio can act as the bulletin board or the reader. As the bulletin board, we can expose some data for all BLE radios and BLE readers. BLE specification also provides notification mechanisms to alert other readers as to when data is changed.

In this chapter, we explore how to work with BLE on Arduino Nano 33 IoT. Next, we set up a BLE library in order to work with BLE radio on Arduino Nano 33 IoT.

# Setting up BLE

To work with BLE on Arduino Nano 33 IoT, we need the ArduinoBLE library. We can perform BLE operations such as making and advertising BLE services. A detail of the ArduinoBLE library can be found at this link, `https://www.arduino.cc/en/Reference/ArduinoBLE`.

You can open the Library Manager dialog from the menu Sketch ➤ Include Library ➤ Manage Libraries. After clicking, you will obtain a dialog, as shown in Figure 6-1.

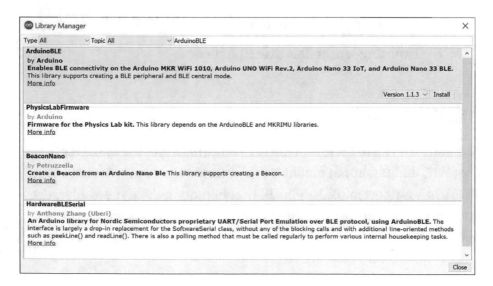

***Figure 6-1.***  *Adding the ArduinoBLE library*

You can type ArduinoBLE in the search textbox. Then, click the ENTER key. You should see the ArduinoBLE library in the result form. Select this library and then install it. After completion, you can build the Arduino program to apply BLE radio.

# Demo 1: Hello Arduino BLE

The first demo is to build a hello world application for BLE radio. We advertise our BLE with a certain BLE name. If the BLE reader is connected, we can turn on LED. When the BLE reader is disconnected, we turn off LED. Next, we write a program with Arduino software.

## Writing Sketch Program

We will develop the Arduino program to advertise the BLE service. We will turn on the LED after the BLE reader is connected. You start by opening Arduino software. Create a new program. Next, we write codes with step-by-step.

First, we import the ArduinoBLE library in our program. We just write this code:

```
#include <ArduinoBLE.h>
```

On the setup() function, we initialize serial communicate, LED, and BLE radio. We call Serial.begin() to initialize serial communication with baudrate 115200. We set the LED pin on LED_BUILTIN as OUTPUT mode. To activate BLE radio on Arduino Nano 33 IoT, we can call the BLE.begin() function.

```
void setup() {
  Serial.begin(115200);
  while (!Serial);

  pinMode(LED_BUILTIN, OUTPUT);
```

```
// begin initialization
if (!BLE.begin()) {
  Serial.println("starting BLE failed!");
  while (1);
}
```

Now we set our BLE radio name by calling BLE.setLocalName(). This name will be detected on the BLE reader. We also set BLE UUID by calling the BLE.setAdvertisedServiceUuid() function. BLE UUID represents a 128-bit value computed. You can generate UUID using this online tool, https://www.guidgenerator.com/online-guid-generator.aspx.

```
BLE.setLocalName("HelloBLE");
BLE.setAdvertisedServiceUuid("19B10000-E8F2-537E-4F6C-
D104768A1214");

// start advertising
BLE.advertise();
Serial.println("Bluetooth device active, waiting for
connections...");
}
```

Make sure your BLE UUID complies with standard BLE SIG. Some BLE UUIDs are reserved by their services. You can check these services at this link, https://www.bluetooth.com/specifications/assigned-numbers/service-discovery/.

Next, we wait for the incoming BLE reader on the loop() function. We can call BLE.contral() to wait for BLE readers.

```
void loop() {
  // wait for a BLE central
  BLEDevice central = BLE.central();
```

After the BLE reader is connected to our BLE radio on Arduino Nano 33 IoT, we can obtain BLEDevice object. Then, we turn on the LED by calling digitalWrite()with passing HIGH value. Then, we perform infinite looping by checking connection status.

```
if (central) {
  Serial.print("Connected to central: ");
  Serial.println(central.address());
  digitalWrite(LED_BUILTIN, HIGH);

  while (central.connected()) {
    // do nothing
  }
```

If the BLE reader is disconnected, we will obtain a false value from central.connected(). After that, we turn off the LED by calling digitalWrite() with passing LOW value.

```
  digitalWrite(LED_BUILTIN, LOW);
  Serial.print("Disconnected from central: ");
  Serial.println(central.address());
  }
}
```

Our program is done. You can save this program as HelloBLE.

## Testing Program

Now our Arduino program, HelloBLE, can be compiled and uploaded to Arduino Nano 33 IoT. To test this program, we need a mobile phone with Android or iOS platform. In this demo, I use an Android phone.

First, open Serial Monitor to see the program output from the HelloBLE program. Next, install nRF Connect for Mobile application on the Google Play store or Apple store. You can see nRF Connect for Mobile application from the Google Play store in Figure 6-2.

Download and install nRF Connect for Mobile application for mobile platforms. After installing, you can run this program. You can see my nRF Connect for Mobile application on Android as shown in Figure 6-3. Next, we can connect to Arduino Nano 33 IoT.

***Figure 6-2.*** *nRF Connect for Mobile application on the Google Play store*

*Figure 6-3.* *A form of nRF Connect for Mobile application*

We can tap SCAN to obtain a list of BLE devices. You should see the HelloBLE service. You can see my HelloBLE in Figure 6-4. If you don't see it, you should tap the SCAN button again.

Now you tap the CONNECT button on HelloBLE. After that, we will connect to Arduino Nano 33 IoT over BLE radio. Figure 6-5 shows my Android phone was connected to the HelloBLE service from Arduino Nano 33 IoT.

To disconnect from the HelloBLE service, you can click the DISCONNECT button. Then, our mobile device closes BLE radio communication. If you already opened the Serial Monitor tool, you will see all event messages on this tool. You can see my program output on the Serial Monitor tool in Figure 6-6.

**Figure 6-4.**  *HelloBLE service is showing*

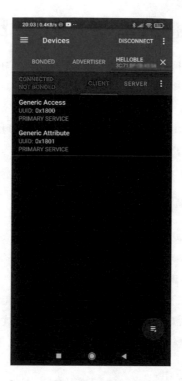

***Figure 6-5.*** *Connected to HelloBLE service*

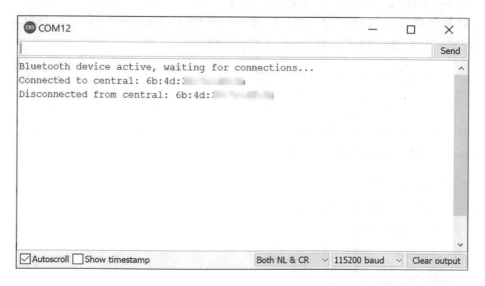

***Figure 6-6.*** *Program output on the serial console from HelloBLE*

# Demo 2: Controlling LED with BLE

In this demo, we build an LED controller over BLE radio. We utilize the BLE service to expose the LED service. We can turn on/off the LED using the mobile application.

For implementation, we use a program sample from Arduino, LED. Next, we develop the Sketch program.

## Writing the Program

We will develop the Arduino program to control the LED over BLE radio. Now you start by opening Arduino software. Create a new program. Next, we write codes with step-by-step.

First, we import the ArduinoBLE library into our program. We also initialize the BLE Service with BLERead and BLEWrite characteristics. We define ledPin for LED_BUILTIN. We write the following codes.

```
#include <ArduinoBLE.h>

BLEService ledService("19B10000-E8F2-537E-4F6C-D104768A1214");
BLEByteCharacteristic switchCharacteristic("19B10001-E8F2-537E-4F6C-D104768A1214", BLERead | BLEWrite);

const int ledPin = LED_BUILTIN;
```

Then, we initialize serial communication and digital OUTPUT mode on the setup() function. We also initialize BLE radio on Arduino Nano 33 IoT using the BLE.begin() function.

```
void setup() {
  Serial.begin(9600);
  while (!Serial);

  // set LED pin to output mode
  pinMode(ledPin, OUTPUT);
```

```
// begin initialization
if (!BLE.begin()) {
  Serial.println("starting BLE failed!");

  while (1);
}
```

Next, we set the BLE service and characteristics using the addCharacteristic() function. We also initialize the characteristic value by calling the writeValue() function.

```
// set advertised local name and service UUID:
BLE.setLocalName("LED");
BLE.setAdvertisedService(ledService);

// add the characteristic to the service
ledService.addCharacteristic(switchCharacteristic);

// add service
BLE.addService(ledService);

// set the initial value for the characeristic:
switchCharacteristic.writeValue(0);
```

After we define our BLE service, we can start to advertise using the BLE.advertise() function. We print a message for information that our BLE is ready to wait for incoming BLE readers.

```
// start advertising
BLE.advertise();

Serial.println("BLE LED Peripheral");
}
```

On the loop() function, we wait for BLE readers. We use BLE.central(). If the BLE reader is connected to Arduino Nano 33 IoT, we will obtain a BLEDevice object.

```
void loop() {
  BLEDevice central = BLE.central();
```

After the BLE reader was connected to Arduino Nano 33 IoT, we print the MAC address from the BLE reader. Then, we perform a looping and wait for input data from the BLE reader using the value() function from the BLE service characteristic. If the user sends data>0, we turn on the LED. Otherwise, we turn off the LED.

```
  if (central) {
    Serial.print("Connected to central: ");
    // print the central's MAC address:
    Serial.println(central.address());

    // while the central is still connected to peripheral:
    while (central.connected()) {
      // if the remote device wrote to the characteristic,
      // use the value to control the LED:
      if (switchCharacteristic.written()) {
        int val = switchCharacteristic.value();
        Serial.println(val);
        if (val>0) {    // any value other than 0
          Serial.println("LED on");
          digitalWrite(ledPin, HIGH);       // will turn the
                                            // LED on

        } else {                            // a 0 value
          Serial.println(F("LED off"));
          digitalWrite(ledPin, LOW);        // will turn the
                                            // LED off

        }
      }
    }
```

Last, we print the message to the serial terminal if the BLE reader disconnects.

```
    Serial.print(F("Disconnected from central: "));
    Serial.println(central.address());
  }
}
```

Our program is done. You can save this program as LED.

## Testing the Program

Now our Arduino program, LED, can be compiled and uploaded to Arduino Nano 33 IoT. To test this program, we need a mobile phone with Android or iOS platform. In this demo, I use an Android phone.

***Figure 6-7.*** *LED service shows in nRF Connect for Mobile application*

First, open Serial Monitor to see program output from the LED
program. Now you can open the nRF Connect for Mobile application
from your platform. You should see the BLE service on this application,
as shown in Figure 6-7. Tap the CONNECT button to connect to Arduino
Nano 33 IoT.

***Figure 6-8.*** *Showing the BLE service characteristics*

After connecting, you will obtain a form, as shown in Figure 6-8. You
can expand the BLE service characteristics. We have two properties: READ
and WRITE.

Tap the WRITE property icon. Then, set a value 15 to turn on the LED,
as shown in Figure 6-9. Tap SEND to send this value. You should see the
LED lighting on Arduino Nano 33 IoT. You also can send 00 to turn off the
LED on the BLE service WRITE, as shown in Figure 6-10.

**Figure 6-9.** *Writing data 15 to turn on the LED*

***Figure 6-10.*** *Writing data 00 to turn off the LED*

If you have already opened the Serial Monitor tool, you will see program output events information. You can see my program output in Figure 6-11.

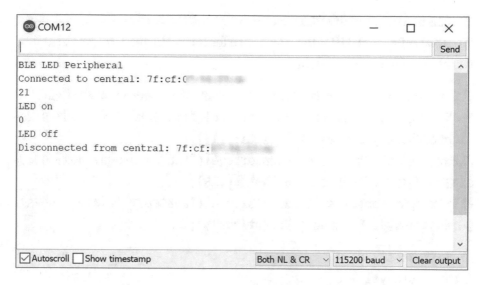

*Figure 6-11.*  *Program output from the LED*

# Demo 3: Sensor Real-Time Monitoring

In this section, we build a sensor real-time monitoring over the BLE radio. We make a BLE service that provides Gyroscope sensor data to the BLE reader. The BLE reader will obtain notification if the sensor data changes.

## Writing the Program

We create a new Arduino program to create the BLE service and then broadcast the Gyroscope sensor to BLE readers. We will create a BLE service with three characteristics. Each BLE characteristic will expose the Gyroscope sensor for x, y, and z degrees.

To start to develop, we can open Arduino software. First, we call the required libraries.

```
#include <ArduinoBLE.h>
#include <Arduino_LSM6DS3.h>
```

Then, we define the BLE service and three BLE characteristics. We need different UUIDs to apply these features. We also define three variables to hold sensor data.

```
BLEService sensorService("16150f38-e7a9-4fe1-ae08-48464baf25b2");
BLEStringCharacteristic  xSensorLevel("ff99948c-18ff-4ed8-942e-
512b9b24b6da", BLERead | BLENotify,15);
BLEStringCharacteristic  ySensorLevel("8084aa6b-6cae-461f-9540-
e1a5768de49d", BLERead | BLENotify,15);
BLEStringCharacteristic  zSensorLevel("ab80cb77-fe74-40d8-9757-
96f8a54c16d9", BLERead | BLENotify,15);

// last sensor data
float oldXLevel = 0;
float oldYLevel = 0;
float oldZLevel = 0;
long previousMillis = 0;
```

On the setup() function, we initialize serial communication with baudrate 115200, the Gyroscope sensor, the LED digital pin, and OLED interintegrated circuit (I2C) display module.

```
void setup() {
  Serial.begin(115200);
  while (!Serial);

  if (!IMU.begin()) {
    Serial.println("Failed to initialize IMU!");
    while (1);
  }
```

```
pinMode(LED_BUILTIN, OUTPUT);

if (!BLE.begin()) {
  Serial.println("starting BLE failed!");
  while (1);
}
```

Now we define the BLE service name and add to the advertised service. Then, add all the BLE characteristics into the BLE service.

```
BLE.setLocalName("Gyroscope");
BLE.setAdvertisedService(sensorService);

sensorService.addCharacteristic(xSensorLevel);
sensorService.addCharacteristic(ySensorLevel);
sensorService.addCharacteristic(zSensorLevel);
BLE.addService(sensorService);
```

We set initial default data on all BLE characteristics using the writeValue() function.

```
xSensorLevel.writeValue(String(0));
ySensorLevel.writeValue(String(0));
zSensorLevel.writeValue(String(0));
```

Now we can start to advertise the BLE service by calling the BLE. advertise() function. BLE readers will recognize this BLE server.

```
BLE.advertise();
Serial.println("Bluetooth device active, waiting for
connections...");
}
```

On the loop() function, we wait for the incoming BLE reader. Once the BLE reader is connected, we print the MAC address of the BLE reader. Then, we turn on the LED.

```
void loop() {
  BLEDevice central = BLE.central();
  if (central) {
    Serial.print("Connected to central: ");
    Serial.println(central.address());
    digitalWrite(LED_BUILTIN, HIGH);
```

If the BLE reader is connected, we have the BLEDevice object. We can perform a looping function until the BLE reader is disconnected. Inside looping, we call the updateGyroscopeLevel() function to update sensor data to the BLE service.

```
    while (central.connected()) {
      //long currentMillis = millis();
      updateGyroscopeLevel();
      delay(300);
    }
```

We turn off the LED after the BLE reader disconnected.

```
    digitalWrite(LED_BUILTIN, LOW);
    Serial.print("Disconnected from central: ");
    Serial.println(central.address());
  }
}
```

For implementation of the updateGyroscopeLevel() function, we read the Gyroscope sensor using IMU.readGyroscope(). We also verify for existing sensor data using the IMU.gyroscopeAvailable() function.

```
void updateGyroscopeLevel() {
  float x, y, z;

  if (IMU.gyroscopeAvailable()) {
    IMU.readGyroscope(x, y, z);
```

We send the Gyroscope sensor data to the BLE service using the writeValue() function. We do this task for all BLE characteristics.

```
if (x != oldXLevel) {
   xSensorLevel.writeValue(String(x));
   oldXLevel = x;
}
if (y != oldYLevel) {
   ySensorLevel.writeValue(String(y));
   oldYLevel = y;
}
if (z != oldZLevel) {
   zSensorLevel.writeValue(String(z));
   oldZLevel = z;
}
Serial.print(x);
Serial.print('\t');
Serial.print(y);
Serial.print('\t');
Serial.println(z);

  }
}
```

Save this program as GyroscopeBLEService.

# Testing

Now we can compile and upload the GyroscopeBLEService program into Arduino Nano 33 IoT board. Next, we can use an nRF Connect for Mobile application. Tap the SCAN button, and you should see a list of the BLE service on your around environment.

Figure 6-12 shows the Gyroscope BLE service detected on an nRF Connect for Mobile application. Then, tap the CONNECT button to connect the Gyroscope BLE service.

After connected, we see properties and characteristics of the Gyroscope BLE service, as shown in Figure 6-13.

***Figure 6-12.*** *Detecting Gyroscope BLE service*

***Figure 6-13.*** *Connected to the Gyroscope BLE service*

You can expand Unknown Service to see the BLE characteristics. After expanded, you will see three BLE characteristics that represent the Gyroscope sensor data. Figure 6-14 shows three BLE characteristics of the Gyroscope BLE service.

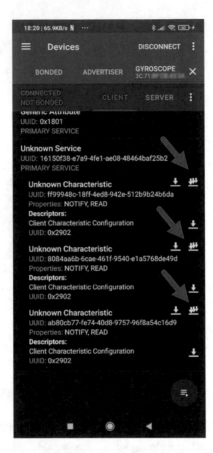

***Figure 6-14.*** *Opening BLE characteristics from the Gyroscope BLE service*

Tap the icon of arrow array, as shown in Figure 6-14. After tapping, you will see sensor data from the Gyroscope sensor. Figure 6-15 shows the Gyroscope sensor data from Arduino Nano 33 IoT. Sensor data is signed by the circle in Figure 6-15.

***Figure 6-15.*** *Showing the Gyroscope sensor over the Gyroscope BLE service*

This is the end of the chapter. You can practice more by creating various BLE services. You also can build your own mobile application to consume BLE services.

# Summary

We have learned how to set up a BLE radio on Arduino Nano 33 IoT board. We also built Arduino programs by applying the BLE radio. We started with developing the Helloworld application. We also controlled the LED over BLE radio.

# Index

© Agus Kurniawan 2021
A. Kurniawan, *Beginning Arduino Nano 33 IoT*,
https://doi.org/10.1007/978-1-4842-6446-1

Printed in the United States
By Bookmasters